101

THE BLUEPRINT FOR A SWANK LIFE

by Olori Swank

Illustrations by *Jerron Couture*

Photos by
Cover Photo & Author Photo: *Allen Cooley*
Pages 8, 9 & 22 : *Aaron Lacey*
Page 35 & 170: *Dewayne Rogers*

Library of Congress Cataloging-in-Publication Data

Printed in the United States of America

ISBN 978-0-9973760-0-5

For More, Visit www.101byOloriSWANK.com

This book is dedicated to my supporters and my support system. Thanks to every one of you for sharing your love with me and lighting up my world.

Table of Contents

Introduction

THE BIGGEST DISSERVICE I DID TO myself in my 20's was assuming I should have had my life figured out. Unfortunately, I know I'm not the only one who has done that. There are so many women in their 20's who think they should have it all "together" before they turn 25. It seems like society trains us to feel that way. When we finish high school, we are supposed to know where we are going to college, and what we will major in. Once we finish college, we are supposed to know what company we will work for and the proper steps we need to take to earn promotions and move up in the ranks at said company. From the day we start work at that company, we are supposed to start planning our retirement; and so on etc.

I graduated high school with honors and college credits from taking AP classes. In my mind, I had it all figured out. I knew I would attend The University of Georgia and major in Biology and Psychology before attending medical school where I would later become a neurosurgeon. I was certain of this. So sure, that the only college I applied to was The University of Georgia. I didn't even bother with applying to any "safety schools." I actually applied using the early admission process and knew before graduating high school that I had been accepted. Like I said, I had it all figured out.

Soon after graduating undergrad, a series of events shocked my pre-planned life and challenged my ideas of needing to have it "figured out." I stumbled upon something else that I loved that gave me great pleasure. I found a career path that made me excited to wake up every morning. At the time, I had no experience in it. As a matter of fact, I had no clue what I was doing; but I was happy doing it. That thing was fashion! Yes, I always had a love for fashion. Yes, I was the girl who used to come to 8am Physics lectures in five-inch stilettos and a tailored suit. Yes, I've definitely been kicked out of an Organic Chemistry lab or two for not having the 'proper attire' (apparently high-heels in lab is a complete no-no). But, when it came to fashion as a career, I didn't even know it was an option. I had no idea I could make a living out of something I saw as just another aspect of my life. To me, fashion and getting dressed up was as rudimentary as brushing my teeth in the morning. I was raised to believe that getting dressed up, and looking presentable is what responsible people do. So imagine my surprise when a friend randomly asked me to be the fashion stylist for a recording artist he had just signed to a major record label. I was flattered. But, when reality sank in that the situation was more than I just doing a friend a favor, I was like a fish in new water. I was thrown into this career with no formal education. It was somewhere in that moment that I realized that the fact of the matter is, we actually have our entire lives to "figure it out." Life is a journey for which we draw the roadmap as we go along; not a destination that's already clearly mapped out for us to follow. I've learned so much on my journey thus far and this book is me sharing those lessons with you. I affectionately named this book *101*, for three reasons:

#1. While attending college at the University of Georgia (go Dawgs!), I noticed that every beginner level subject ended with the numbers "101." I'm sure it is typical at majority of colleges/universities that the beginner course of every subject typically ends with the numbers 101. This book will give you a lot of beginner level information on different topics that women face in the world. From how to organize your closet, to how to prepare for your first date. From what to expect when first launching a business, to the importance of credit and how to keep your credit in excellent shape. I even include ways to handle negativity and trolls you may encounter on social media.

#2. This book is a one on one conversation between me the writer, and you the reader. Many questions that I answer in this book are candid. They are things I never really discuss openly. People are so used to me discussing my career as a fashion stylist, or the ways in which to launch your own eBoutique. I am rarely ever in an open forum where I get to give my take on how I juggle running my business, maintaining a healthy long distance relationship, and how I keep my blue-hued locks so shiny. Unless you follow me on Snapchat, you really don't get a glimpse into my personal life or "sophisti-ratchet" tendencies.

#3. Lastly, the 101 represents the number of questions, answers and tips that I'll be sharing in this guide. Each entry has been categorized by chapters, making it easy for you to reference.

I truly hope you enjoy.

101 Random Things About Me

---

1. My favorite color is not blue. I love heather gray, and black & white combos.

2. If mirror, Lucite and chrome were colors, they would be my favorite.

3. I'd rock gold jewelry over silver any day.

4. I can't leave the house without my diamond stud earrings. I only take them off to clean them. They're a security blanket for me.

5. I didn't go to fashion school. I was a science major.

6. I was in a ton of honor societies in college. I'm kind of a nerd.

7. I am the oldest of three kids—one brother and one sister.

8. I love science and math. Hate English and history.

9. Jeopardy is my favorite show of all time.

10. I am terrified to eat any kind of fried egg; yet I love hard-boiled eggs... and I make an amazing omelet. Weird, huh?

11. I started reading at age 2.

12. I didn't take my first steps until the night of my first birthday. I could talk before I could walk.

13. My Favorite Bag is my Maxi Chanel Double Flap Bag. It's the first Chanel bag I ever bought myself and it cost me $6K.

14. I've lived in Africa (Nigeria), Europe (London, England), and North America.

15. I was born in Washington, D.C.

16. I learned how to drive a stick shift when I was around 12-13 years old.

17. Up until I graduated from undergrad, I always wanted to be a neurosurgeon.

18. I am terrified of heights.

19. Thanksgiving is my favorite holiday. I'd trade my birthday for two Thanksgivings a year.

20. I have an unhealthy crush on Bane from *Dark Knight Rises.* Something about the mask and the voice makes me want to lose my religion.

21. I have a newfound obsession with Snapchat. I find myself pausing every time something amazing happens like "I have to snap this."

22. I wear heels almost everyday; but I own over 150 pairs of sneakers.

23. Sometimes, I binge on episodes of *Shark Tank*.

24. My blue hair is the result of a dye-job accident that I decided to stick with.

25. My hair has been blue for almost 10 years straight.

26. I've taken almost 10 years of French classes and still can't speak it worth a lick.

27. I'm fluent in Yoruba though. I can speak, read, and write it.

28. In fifth grade I elected to take Arabic as my foreign language.

29. My fridge is more organized than a lot of people's planners.

30. I have an affinity for stationary and office supplies.

31. I don't like milk.

32. I've never broken a bone.

33. I played soccer in high school – I wasn't very good. LOL

34. Growing up, I was the most spoiled child but the most disciplined child at the same time.

35. As a young child, I used to sell the pages of my coloring book to the kids in the neighborhood for a quarter.

36. I am an introvert.

37. I read anatomy books for fun.

38. I love memorizing elements from the periodic table.

39. I have yet to become one of those people who like working out.

40. Cooking is one of my favorite hobbies.

41. I am not as high maintenance as I appear.

42. I experiment constantly with nail designs on my fingers; but my toes are always soft pink. ...or white if I'm feeling daring.

43. I have two cell phones: an iPhone 5 & iPhone 6.

44. I have two iPads. I don't use either one. They sit in a drawer in my bedroom.

45. I hate sour cream and onion chips. I prefer the plain ones.

46. I hate peanut butter.

47. Cashews are the only kind of nuts I like.

48. Apple pie is my favorite pie.

49. I love cotton candy.

50. I've seen the movie *Casino* 100 times and still watch it like I've never seen it before.

51. *Scarface, Sex And The City, Love & Other Disasters*, and *Despicable Me* are a few of my other favorite movies.

52. I love football. I'm not really into basketball as much.

53. My favorite football team is the Cowboys.

54. My favorite basketball team is the Lakers.

55. I'm a total daddy's girl.

56. I don't really like Chocolate Chip Cookies. I prefer Oatmeal Raisin Cookies.

57. The possibility of me crying during an episode of *Undercover Bosses* is extremely high.

58. I like tall guys. I joke that my height requirement is 6'6; but that I'll settle for 6'2".

59. My boyfriend nicknamed me "Smurf."

60. My favorite mode of transportation is an airplane.

61. I buy all my plane tickets the day before the flight. Buying them too far in advance freaks me out.

62. I can never keep track of how many tattoos I have.

63. I love getting tattoos but I hate getting piercings.

64. I keep way too many tabs and windows open on my Internet browser

65. I never turn off or restart my laptop. It's so bad.

66. I'd much rather be cold than hot.

67. I don't really watch TV. I watch an average of an hour a week. ... unless I'm binging on a *Shark Tank* marathon.

68. I'm obsessed with Zaxby's. The 'Wings & Things Platter' is my vice.

69. When I find that one thing I like at a restaurant, I'll order it repeatedly and only go to the restaurant for that one thing. I'm more likely to try a new restaurant than I am to try a new dish at a restaurant I already go to.

70. I love seafood.

71. The only time I really eat pork is when I eat bacon.

72. Food makes me happy.

73. I love kids.

74. I want three kids—two boys and a girl, in that order.

75. I'm the lame one out of my siblings. They still pick on me for being nerdy.

76. I am friendly to everyone; but I only have a handful of friends.

77. I have never cheated on a boyfriend.

78. I am loyal to a fault.

79. I hate cardio. I prefer weightlifting. I would have leg day everyday at the gym if I could.

80. I don't smoke.

81. I drink socially. The Moscow Mule is one of my favorite cocktails.

82. I prefer a high-rise condo to a house.

83. Prefer foreign cars to American.

84. Even though I was born in Washington D.C., I claim Atlanta, GA as home.

85. I currently live in Los Angeles, and have lived here for 4 years.

86. 13 is my favorite and lucky number.

87. I am a Pisces. Birthday: March 13.

88. I wear a US women's size 9, but I'm a 40 in European shoes.

89. I love God and Trap Music.

90. I don't listen to R&B Music.

91. Tasha Cobbs is my favorite Gospel Singer.

92. Mark Cuban, Jay-Z, and Warren Buffet are amongst my favorite entrepreneurs.

93. I want to build a school in Africa one day.

94. I don't have any pets.

95. I only joined Instagram because I wanted cool filters for my photos. I had no idea it was a social media platform at first.

96. I'm a total germophobe.

97. All the cash in my wallet has to face the same way and be in ascending order.

98. I hate sitting on row 1 on a plane. Either window seat on row 3 is my preferred seat.

99. I hate being late for anything.

100. People who ask me too many questions irritate the life out of me.

> *101. I'm on a constant quest to be better today than I was yesterday."*

CHAPTER 1

Fashion & Style

> " Fashion is not something that exists in dresses only. Fashion is in the sky, in the street, fashion has to do with ideas, the way we live, what is happening."
>
> —*Coco Chanel*

1. *What are staple items every woman should have in her wardrobe?*

At some point, every woman has uttered the phrase, "I have nothing to wear." We've all said it; some of you are probably thinking it right now. The fact is, you have a ton of options. You just need to have the proper essentials to tie it together. Here are a few staples every woman should have in her closet.

- Black Suit (comprised of black pants and a sharp blazer)
- Pencil Skirt
- LBD (little black dress)
- White Collar Dress Shirt
- High-end T-Shirt
- Dark Denim Jeans
- Trench Coat (Khaki or Black)
- Wool Coat
- Leather Jacket
- Classic Black Pumps
- Nude Pumps
- Ballet Flats
- Leather Daytime Bag
- Evening Clutch
- Great Pair of Sunglasses That Suit Your Face

" The fact is, you have a ton of options."

2. What items are good to save on and what items are good to splurge on?

It's best to splurge on items that will:

I. Give you a lot of wear.

II. Hold their value over the course of time.

III. Be staple pieces that aren't likely to go out of style soon.

For example, it's better to splurge on a great leather jacket that you can wear repeatedly for years, versus splurging on a pair of bell-bottom jeans. Although those jeans might be in style now, they're very likely to not be in style next year. On the same token, a leather jacket is a staple piece. Your staple pieces will come in handy when mixing-and-matching with the trend items to create looks in your closet, so you want to make sure they're high quality so they can last a long time.

Also it's ok to splurge on jewelry and other items you can pass down to your daughter, nieces, etc. My favorite thing to splurge on is a Chanel handbag. Chanel not only has a proven track record of holding its value over the years, but they actually increase in value. No matter the status of the economy, Chanel prices have never gone down. Did you know the cost of a medium Chanel classic flap bag in 1990 was $1,150, today it's $4,900 for the same bag. With the consistent price increases, Chanel

bags are becoming just as good as real estate when it comes to making an investment (or at least that's what I like to tell myself at the register to feel better about seeing a comma on my receipts). Even so, it's wise to only splurge on the classic/iconic styles like the flap bag. Even a Chanel piece that is 'trendy' can prove to be a not so great investment.

You should totally save on items that are trendy, or popular. I've seen so many trends come and go for so long that I know even the most electrifying trends will die off soon after they peak. So if something is the latest "OMG, I've gotta have it" hot-ticket item in the fashion streets, find a more affordable alternative. You're going to be so upset when those leggings with the suspenders you spent $800 on are no longer cool to wear.

> " *You should totally save on items that are trendy, or popular.*"

3. *What is the best way to organize your closet?*

Want to be able to get dressed quicker in the morning, keep your room cleaner longer, and freak out less about having nothing to wear? If you answered yes, do yourself a favor and organize your closet. Organizing your closet will make your life so much easier. When you can see all your clothes in front of you in an organized fashion, you'll be able to move through your closet with the same amount of finesse Neo uses to move through the Matrix. When you organize your closet, everything will finally make sense and your wardrobe options will broaden immensely.

The first step to a well-organized closet is to purge your closet (we'll talk more about how to do this in the next section). You will need as much space as you can, so holding on to items that you can no longer fit, don't need, or don't like is a definite NO!

The second step is to find the best storage solution system that works for you. Whether it's ELFA systems, which you can find at The Container Store and Ikea, or hiring a company, like CaliforniaClosets.com to build you a custom closet. The proper storage system is essential to the organization process.

Once your closet has been purged and you have shelving, and racks, etc. in place, you can move on to the arranging process.

Start off by arranging your clothes by type. Section off your dresses, skirts, pants, tops, and coats. Once you've done that you want to subdivide each section. For example, subdivide your pants section by jeans, cargos, trousers, etc. Once you've subdivided them by style, go back in and arrange them by color (going from light to dark). When deciding on where to place each category, it's important for you to keep your everyday-wear within closest reach. Items like eveningwear or suits (if you don't wear a suit to work daily) can be placed away from your everyday reach.

> " *The first step to a well-organized closet is to purge your closet.*"

> **If you haven't worn it in six months to a year, it's time to let it go.**

4. What is the proper way to purge your closet?

The proper way to purge your closet is to find which items you have not worn in six months to a year. If you haven't worn it in six months to a year, it's time to let it go. You should also look at items that are too small or too big since nine times out of ten, if they don't fit, you will not wear them. Don't fool yourself with the excuse, "I'll grow into it" or, "I'll lose weight for it."

Another question to ask yourself is, "What's the likelihood I'll ever wear that item again?" A lot of us have items in our closet that we love; they are so memorable, unique, and distinctive but we are embarrassed to be caught wearing them twice. Unless it's an item that holds extreme sentimental value, like a wedding dress or a vintage sweater passed down from your grandmother, let it go. You should also get rid of any items that are damaged, or don't represent your current style of dress.

If a zipper is broken or a button is missing, and you've been saying for the longest time that you were going to get it fixed, and you've yet to get it fixed, most likely you are not going to wear that item again. There's no need to leave it in your closet taking up space when it's not even in the best condition for you to pull out and put on if you feel like wearing it. Ask yourself if you were in the mall shopping right now and you were standing in front of this item, would you buy it? If the answer is no, then it is time to let that item go.

It's not uncommon for us to love something in the store, buy it, get home, never wear it and then not like it anymore. Don't let buyer's remorse be the reason you keep something in your closet especially when you don't intend to wear it. You can donate those items to a battered women's shelter and feel just as good about yourself as the day you bought it. Remember, one woman's "yikes, I hate this," is another woman's "oh my God, I love this."

Lastly, ask yourself if you feel comfortable in an item. If the last time you wore that dress you broke out in hives in front of a dinner party of twenty people, the likelihood of you wearing that dress again no matter how cute it is slim to none.

Once you've decided what to get rid of, decide what to do with it. For high-end items, like Dolce and Gabbana, or Yves Saint Laurent, I take them to local consignment stores. This is a great way to get back some of the money you spent towards the item while giving you some pocket money to spend on new duds. When doing consignment, remember to discuss your options with the consigner. Some consignment shops pay you flat out for your goods. Others hold on to the items and pay if they sell. Every consignment's pay/commission structure is different, so be clear on the terms before you engage in business with them. For the items I do not consign, I like to donate them to women's shelters, churches, and Goodwill. I also make sure to get a tax-deductible receipt that I can use for a future tax write-off.

> " *Once you've decided what to get rid of, decide what to do with it.* "

5. *How can you get the most wear out of each item?*

The key to recycling your pieces is to begin to see them as more than what they're intended to be. — For example, a dress can be a skirt and a top too.

**One dress,
five ways**

I

2

3   4   5

Apple   Hourglass   Pear   Rectangle   Petite

6. How to dress for your body type

Let's face it; all bodies are not built equally. Although I would love nothing more than to say any girl can wear anything, the truth of the matter is some styles are just way more flattering on certain body types. When it comes to looking sharp, no one body type is better than the other. The key to being stylish is dressing for your body. Here are a few tips on what to look for and what to avoid for your body type.

❝ *Some styles are just way more flattering on certain body types.*❞

BODY TYPE: *Apple*

Characteristics: Wider mid-section, broad shoulders, full bust, wide waist, and wide upper back, top-heavy. The majority of your weight is housed at the center of your body. Arms and legs tend to be smaller in comparison. The goal is to draw attention away from the mid-section, while simultaneously creating a more defined waistline.

Famous Apple Celebs: Oprah, Jill Scott, Angelina Jolie, Tyra Banks.

What to wear: Structured jackets, a-line skirts, lean-streamlined jackets.

What to avoid: Low cut bottoms (shorts, jeans, or pants), crop tops, turtle necks, and wide shoulder fitting tops.

BODY TYPE: *Hourglass*

Characteristics: Full bust, curvy hips, small waist. This body type looks like an hourglass. The goal here is to show off your curves, not to hide them. Just be careful not to show too much because this body type is already very alluring so it's easy to appear overly sexy and reveal too much.

Famous Hourglass Celebs: Kim Kardashian, Marilyn Monroe, Jennifer Lopez, Nicki Minaj.

What to wear: Wrap dresses, clothing belted at the waist, pencil skirts, bodycon dresses, crop tops with high-waisted bottoms.

What to avoid: Oversized, shapeless, or boxy garments, shift-dresses, tunics, oversize cardigans, and boyfriend jeans.

BODY TYPE: Pear

Characteristics: Petite upper body, small shoulders and bust, wider hips and backside. The goal is to balance out your body by drawing more attention to your top half, and giving the illusion of a more elongated body.

Famous Pear Celebs: Beyonce, Kate Winslet, Shakira.

What to wear: Structured jackets, a-line skirts, off shoulder tops, bomber jackets, wide V or sweetheart neck tops, wide sleeve tops.

What to avoid: Cigarette-style or too-tight pants. Avoid tops that end mid-thigh because these draw attention to your hips and bottom areas making them look wider.

BODY TYPE: Rectangle

Characteristics: No curves. The silhouette is pretty much straight up and down. The shoulder, bust, waist and hips are about the same ratio.

Famous Rectangle Celebs: Victoria Beckham, Sarah Jessica Parker, Gabrielle Union, Kelly Rowland.

What to wear: High-necked tops that give the appearance of a fuller chest, slightly flared trousers, skirts with box-pleats. If you're feeling daring and adventurous, you can play with androgynous styles by employing chic tailored separates.

What to avoid: Sweetheart necklines, oversized tunics, and baggy pants.

BODY TYPE: Petite

Characteristics: Being petite mostly has to do with your height. If you're under 5'4, many places will consider you 'petite'. It's very possible to be petite and also be another body-type. For example, you can be a petite-hourglass. The goal with dressing for a petite figure is to find items that don't overpower or overshadow your small frame.

Famous Petite Celebs: Jada Pinkett-Smith, Eva Longoria, Lady Gaga, Adrienne Bailon.

What to wear: V-neck tops that elongate your neck, wrap dresses, empire waist dresses, mini skirts.

What to avoid: Oversized garments, wide leg trousers, midi dresses, Bermuda shorts.

7. Dress how you want to be addressed

Fashion is a powerful form of expression. It's how you introduce yourself without saying a word. Being stylish and fashionable is great. However, it's important to learn how to dress for every occasion. If you're going to Sunday Brunch, you don't want to be dressed as if you're about to walk the red carpet at the Oscars. If you're going to a black tie soiree, showing up in your cutest cocktail dress will most likely catch some side-eyes.

8. My personal favorite online shopping sites

1. SWANKblue.com
2. LuisaViaRoma.com
3. HLorenzo.com
4. NastyGal.com
5. Saks.com
6. Asos.com
7. Topshop.com
8. Zara.com
9. Uniqlo.com
10. Target.com
11. Baublebar.com

> " *Fashion is a powerful form of expression.* "

CHAPTER 2

All Things Beauty

" There are no ugly women, only lazy ones."
—*Helena Rubinstein*

9. What's your key to clear skin?

I'll be honest and say I've been blessed with naturally good skin. I've never had to combat acne or troubled-skin; but I will share with you my secrets to maintaining my skin.

Drink plenty of water!

Staying hydrated is a MAJOR key to having clear skin. Try to drink at least eight 8-oz glasses of water a day. Make sure you consume more water than you do sugary drinks like soda. Sugar is not your skin's friend. The last thing you want to be is dehydrated. Dehydration causes your skin to produce more oils when it's dry, and this may cause you to break out.

Develop a skin-care regiment and stick to it

The most basic regiment is: cleanse, tone, moisturize (exfoliating once or twice a week depending on how sensitive your skin is). You should cleanse, tone, and moisturize twice a day; once in the morning before applying makeup, and once at night before going to bed. Determine your skin-type and use products that are best for the type of skin you have. I have normal skin and I've found that Neutrogena Daily Foaming face wash, Toner, and Daily moisturizing face cream (SPF 15) work well for me. Once you

find products that work for your skin, stick to them. Once your skin gets use to something, changing products can sometimes cause your skin to act up. ...And don't forget the SPF! Using a daily moisturizer and/ or daily sunscreen with an SPF of at least fifteen will help prevent wrinkles and dark spots.

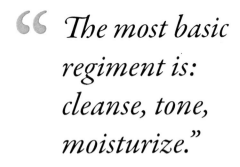

The most basic regiment is: cleanse, tone, moisturize.

Wash your face properly

Wash your face with lukewarm to cold water. Scalding hot water may cause skin irritation. Also, be sure to wash your hands before washing your face. Transferring bacteria, dirt, and oil from your hands to your face while washing defeats the purpose. Wash your hands with antibacterial soap first and then use your daily face wash. I use my hands to scrub my face, but if you are using a washcloth, just make sure you're using a clean washcloth EVERY time. Do not use the same washcloth you've used all day to dry your hands on your face; you can transfer bacteria that way as well.

Clean Your Makeup Brushes & Clean Out Your Makeup Bag

Brushes are a breeding-ground for bacteria. Using your makeup brushes without properly cleaning them is an easy way to transfer bacteria to your face, which will cause breakouts. You should wash your makeup brushes every two weeks at the very least. Use a mild antibacterial soap (like Dawn) and warm water to clean your brushes. Lay them flat to prevent your brushes from becoming misshaped.

It's also important to discard old makeup. Most makeup has a shelf life of 6 months from the day you open it. Anything you've had longer than six months will most likely contain bacteria and should be thrown away.

Don't Sleep or Workout With Makeup On

This is the toughest one for me. I'm usually so exhausted when my day is over. The last thing I want to do before bed is wash my face. But it must be done! Not only does sleeping in makeup add years to your face, it clogs your pores and prevents your skin from breathing and going through it's natural rejuvenation process while you sleep.

If you find yourself too tired to wash your face at night, keep makeup remover wipes on your nightstand. My favorite wipes are Neutrogena Makeup remover wipes. They are gentle on my face, but strong enough to remove even the most stubborn makeup (especially the waterproof stuff).

It's also really important to remove makeup before working out too. When your makeup mixes with your sweat during a workout it can clog your pores. It's a total recipe for a breakout.

I use only white washcloths and pillowcases that have been laundered in hot water with bleach. I never use anything color dyed on my face nor do I sleep on colored pillowcases. Sometimes, something as simple as the dye in the fabric will cause your face to be irritated, and I'm just not willing to take the risk. Fragrances from detergent can also cause skin irritation so I avoid them. Be sure to change your pillowcases weekly. Things like oil from your hair and dead skin cells can build up on your pillows and cause your skin to breakout.

Don't Touch Your Face & Don't Pop Zits!

As I said before, you don't want to transfer bacteria, oil, and dirt from your hands onto your face, so keep your hands away from your face. This means you shouldn't randomly rub your face throughout the day or place your face in your palms. Because our hands are one of the dirtiest parts of our body, the less you touch your face throughout the day, the better. You should also try to keep other people from touching your face as well. Many people affectionately touch other people's faces not thinking about where their hands have been. You don't want their bacteria on your face. If you're getting makeup done or spa-services, make sure the person performing the service washes their hands.

And whatever you do, if you have a zit, do not pop it! Popping zits can cause scars.

10. Some of my Favorite Do It Yourself Beauty Recipes

Aspirin-Honey Face Mask

This mask is great for exfoliating skin. I love it because after five minutes of leaving it on you will already see the results of smoother, clearer, rejuvenated skin.

INGREDIENTS:

4 Uncoated, Plain Aspirin* Pills (the generic store brand usually works best)

1 Tablespoon Warm Water

2 Tablespoons Raw Honey

DIRECTIONS:

Combine aspirin and water to dissolve the pills and form a paste. Mix in the honey. Apply a thin layer of the mixture on your face, and then allow it to dry. Let it sit for 5 minutes then rinse away with warm water, using gentle circular motions.

* If you're allergic to aspirin, Do Not Use This Mask!

Lemonade Face Scrub

This lemonade face scrub is one of my favorites to apply before bed. It too only takes 5 minutes to see results. When I wash it off, my skin is brighter and smoother. Not to mention, it is very hydrating and gives you an insane glow.

INGREDIENTS:

1 Lemon

2 Tablespoons Organic Sugar

1 Tablespoon Raw Honey

1 Tablespoon Olive Oil

DIRECTIONS:

1. Squeeze one lemon into a bowl and remove the seeds

2. Add sugar and honey

3. Rub olive oil into your skin before applying the lemonade scrub to your face using circular motions

4. Let the scrub set on your face for 5 minutes

5. Rinse skin and apply a moisturizing face cream

11. Beauty detox recipes

What you ingest can play a major role in the complexion of your skin. Here are a few of my favorite recipes that have my skin glowing from the inside out:

ACV Shot

This isn't so much as recipe as it is a quick wellness shot. Apple cider vinegar helps balance your pH level thereby yielding clearer skin. Try drinking a tablespoon of Apple Cider Vinegar daily for clear, acne-free skin.

Glowing Green Smoothie

INGREDIENTS:

    1 cup water

    12 ounces romaine lettuce

    8 ounces of spinach

    4 celery stalks

    1 green apple, sliced

    1 pear, sliced

    1 banana

    ½ lemon, peeled

DIRECTIONS:

Combine water, romaine, spinach, celery, and blend until smooth. Then add apple, pear, banana, and lemon. Blend until smooth. Enjoy!

Glowing Skin Elixir:

INGREDIENTS:

    1 Cucumber

    2 Green Apples

    2 Celery stalks

    2 Pineapple Slices

    1 Cup Mint leaves

DIRECTIONS:

Combine cucumber, green apples, celery, pineapple, and mint in a blender, and blend until smooth. Enjoy!

12. *Favorite Foundations, Concealers, and Setting Powders*

FOUNDATIONS

Estee Lauder Double Wear Foundation (I wear the shade: "Sandalwood")

Revlon Colorstay Makeup (I wear "Cappuccino" and "Caramel" mixed)

Makeup Forever Ultra HD Invisible Cover Foundation (I wear "180 = r530 – brown")

CONCEALERS

LA Girl Pro Conceal HD Concealer (I wear: "Toast" and "Fawn" mixed)

MAC Cosmetics Pro Longwear Concealer (I wear: "NW40" and "NC45" mixed)

Kevyn Aucoin the Sensual Skin Enhancer, (I wear: "SX 12")

SETTING POWDERS (HIGHLIGHT)

Laura Mercier Translucent Loose Setting Powder

Ben Nye Luxury Powder – 'Banana'

NYX Cosmetics Studio Finishing Powder Translucent Finish

13. *Favorite Drugstore Products*

Neutrogena makeup remover cleansing towelettes – removes the toughest makeup (even waterproof stuff). I swear by these wipes.

Neutrogena Fresh Foaming Cleanser

Neutrogena Alcohol-Free Toner

Neutrogena Healthy Skin Face Lotion with sunscreen SPF 15

Revlon Colorstay Skinny Liquid Liner (in "Blackout") – I'm obsessed with wingtip eyeliner and this liquid liner is my secret weapon for getting the perfectly precise wing eyeliner

L'Oreal Infallible Eye Liner (in "Blacknoir") – I use this liner on my lower rim

Black Opal Foundation Stick – I use these mostly for highlighting ("Truly Topaz") or contouring ("Black Walnut")

Revlon Colorstay Makeup (I wear "cappuccino" and "caramel" mixed)

LA Girl Pro Conceal HD Concealer (I wear: 'toast' and 'fawn' mixed)

Maybelline® Volum' Express® The Colossal Mascara

Ardell Professional Double Up Wispies False Eyelashes

Sally Hansen Salon Effects Real Nail Polish Strips

BEFORE

LINE BELOW

LINE ABOVE

BLEND

DEFINE

FINISHED LOOK

14. Brows on Fleek

Products I use:

Anastasia Dip Brow (in "Chocolate")

Makeup Addiction Cosmetics Angled Brow Brush

MAC Cosmetics Studio Finish SPF35 Concealer (in "NW40")

MAC Cosmetics 212 Flat Definer Brush Products

Anastasia Tinted Brow Gel (in "warm dark brown")

Directions:

Dip the angled brow brush into the Dip Brow. Saturate the brush with just enough product to coat the bottom of the brush bristles. A little of this product goes a long way. It's better to build it on slowly than to pile it all on at once.

Use brush to draw a defined line underneath the brow.

Without going back for more product, use the brush to draw a defined line on the outer ¾ of the top of the brow. Make sure the ends of the bottom line and top line connect to form a clean tail at the end of your brow.

Use a brow brush, spoolie, or even a toothbrush (I prefer the toothbrush) to brush the dip brow color through the brows. This will fill in any sparse areas and blend any harsh lines.

Now, you can go back in and add more product (if necessary) to fill any sparse areas that remain throughout your brow. Remember to brush again after adding more product to blend out any harsh lines.

For a more natural look, focus on adding the majority of the product to the outer ¾ of the brow.

Once you're done filling in sparse areas, define the brow further by using the 212 MAC Cosmetics brush to apply the Studio Finish concealer under the brow. Using a concealer two shades lighter than your skin will give the illusion of a freshly waxed and super defined brow.

Be sure to blend out the concealer removing any harsh lines. Finish by setting the brows with brow gel.

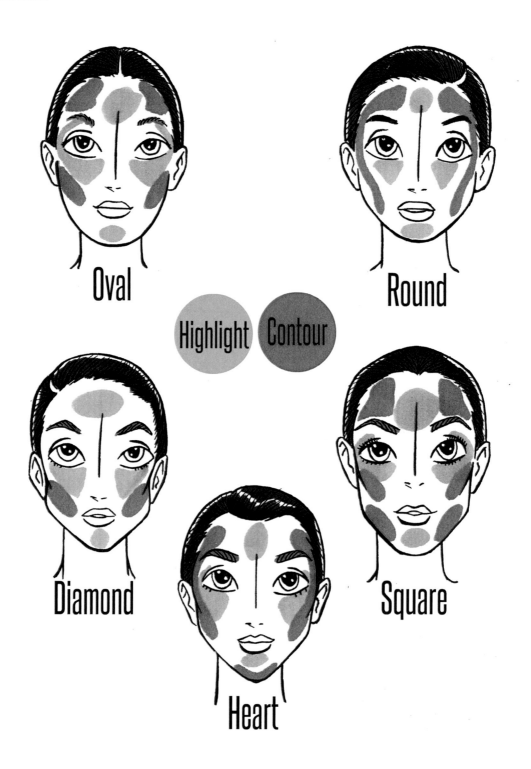

Oval

Round

Highlight Contour

Diamond

Heart

Square

15. How to Contour and Highlight Your Face

Nowadays, one thing that almost every girl covets is a BEAT FACE! With the influx of YouTube tutorials and Instagram gurus, one would think this would be an easy task, right? Wrong! With so much information at our disposal and no real authorities policing all the advice, it's made it even harder to know who is doing it right and whom to take advice from. Luckily, for you, I'm here to break it down in a simple, foolproof way.

So what exactly is contouring? Contouring is a technique used to reshape, define, or recede an area (like your cheekbones, nose, forehead). You achieve this by applying a matte product that is two shades darker than your skin tone to the area. You can use foundation sticks, cream-based makeup, and/or powders.

Highlighting in a sense is the opposite of contouring. Highlighting, as the word itself states, is intended to 'highlight' or accentuate certain features. You want to highlight the high points of your face. The high points are the areas of your face that catch the most natural light. You achieve the perfect highlight by using a product that is two shades lighter than your skin tone. The product most commonly used is concealer. However, foundation sticks, cream-based makeup, and/or powders can be used as well.

To help you further, I've included cool highlight-contour maps on page 24 for you to follow based on your face shape.

Diamond Face Shape

Characteristics: The most notable characteristic of a diamond shaped face is a hairline narrower than the checks. Also, if your face is longer than it is wide, and your jawline meets at a slightly pointed chin, then you are a diamond.

Apply Contour: To get the best contour, apply product to the area right below your cheekbones. Start from your ear and go the length of half your cheek.

Apply Highlight: To get the best highlight, apply product in an inverted triangle shape to the area right under your eyes. Also apply in an oval shape to the middle of your forehead; and a circle shape in on the middle of your chin.

Heart Face Shape

Characteristics: The most notable characteristic of a heart shaped face is a widow's peak. For this face shape, your cheeks are a tad wider than your hairline and the jawline meets at a slightly pointed chin.

Apply Contour: To get the best contour, apply product to the temples and sides of your forehead. Also apply to the area right below your cheekbones, starting from your ear and going the length of about half your cheek. You should also apply to the bottom of your chin to broaden it a little.

Apply Highlight: To get the best highlight, apply product in an inverted triangle shape to the area right under your eyes. Also apply to the outer corner of your brow bone, middle of your forehead; and the middle of your chin.

Oval Face Shape

Characteristics: The most notable characteristic of an Oval shaped face is that it resembles an upside down egg. There are no real defined points on this face shape; not at the hairline, nor at the chin. For this face shape, your face is about two-thirds longer than it is wide.

Apply Contour: To get the best contour, apply product to the sides of your forehead. Also apply to the area right below your cheekbones, starting from your ear and going the length of about half your cheek.

Apply Highlight: To get the best highlight, apply product in an inverted triangle shape to the area right under your eyes. Also apply to middle of your forehead, and the middle of your chin.

Round Face Shape

Characteristics: The most notable characteristic of a round shaped face is that it has the same length and width. There are no real defined points on this face shape either; not at the hairline, nor at the chin.

Apply Contour: To get the best contour, apply product to the temples and sides of your forehead. Also apply to the area right below your cheekbones, starting from your ear and going the length of about half your cheek. You should also apply to the bottom of your jawline to make your face appear slightly longer.

Apply Highlight: To get the best highlight, apply product in an inverted triangle shape to the area right under your eyes. Also apply to the outer corner of your brow bone, middle of your forehead, and the middle of your chin.

Square Face Shape

Characteristics: The most notable characteristic of a square shaped face is similar to a round face in that this face shape has the same length and width. The difference is that this face has defined points along the hairline and at thee corners of the chin.

Apply Contour: To get the best contour, apply product to the sides of your forehead. Also apply to the area right below your cheekbones starting from your ear and going the length of about half your cheek. You should also apply to the bottom of your jawline to make your face appear narrower.

Apply Highlight: To get the best highlight, apply product in an inverted triangle shape to the area right under your eyes. Also apply to the middle of your forehead and the middle of your chin.

❝ *I'm here to break it down in a simple, foolproof way.*❞

CHAPTER 3

Hair

" Sure, my life isn't perfect, but my hair is, and that's what really matters."

—Unknown

When it comes to hair, we are either trying to get it to grow in some places (like on our heads, or your eyebrows after a horrific wax session) or we are trying to eliminate it from growing altogether in other places (like upper lip, legs and bikini areas). Lets talk about our options for the latter first.

16. Razor, vs Wax, vs Tweeze, vs Thread, vs Laser

Razor: this is probably the cheapest, most accessible alternative. It's as simple as buying a razor and some shaving cream from your local drugstore. The thing I hate about razors though, are razor bumps and the occasional nicks you might receive from shaving in a hurry. Plus, the hair grows back a lot faster. But, this method is fast and doesn't require scheduling an appointment at your local med spa. I recommend it for legs only.

Wax: waxing keeps the hair off longer than shaving, but can be a painful alternative compared to razors. It's all about your pain tolerance. I've had friends who say waxing doesn't hurt. I also have friends who swear away from waxing because it feels like death.

I like how smooth the skin feels after a wax in comparison to shaving. I recommend waxing for your upper lip, eyebrows, and bikini area.

Tweeze: I recommend tweezing for smaller areas like your eyebrows, where detailed precision is needed. However, it can be very time-consuming if you plan on tweezing areas that have a lot of hair. Imagine having to tweeze each individual hair from your legs. Sounds like a nightmare, huh?

Thread: threading is a personal favorite of mine when it comes to my eyebrows. It lasts longer than waxing, and is just as precise as tweezing. It's the best of both worlds and definitely my go to when I want my eyebrows on fleek. Before I invested in laser hair removal, I used to get my upper lip threaded too. Again, it all depends on your sensitivity, but personally, I don't think threading is more painful than waxing.

Laser hair removal is a more permanent solution. My skin is very sensitive to razor use; ingrown hairs and razor bumps were just not a good look under my armpits and bikini line. I was tired of getting waxed all the time, so I opted for a more permanent solution in laser hair removal.

For some, laser hair removal doesn't hurt at all. For others, it's very painful. My therapist told me that lasering darker skin usually hurts more than people with fair skin. I describe laser hair removal as being popped repeatedly with a slightly-hot, tiny rubber band. It's slightly painful, but definitely not unbearable, and totally worth it. If you decide to invest in laser hair removal, it is very important to understand that you will have to undergo multiple sessions in order to stop the hair from growing completely. This can prove to be a little costly, so make sure you save up for it if need be. The typical cost for a laser hair removal session is between $100-$450 depending on the area of the body being treated. Most areas of your body will require anywhere from four to ten treatments/sessions. Each session can take anywhere from 15 minutes to an hour depending on how many areas are being treated. The sessions will need to be four to six weeks apart, so make sure you budget your time as well. Be sure to have a consultation with a laser hair removal specialist before committing to the process.

Now that we've gotten the hair removal options out of the way, let's talk about what we can do to promote hair growth.

17. My Favorite Do It Yourself Hair Treatments

With all the weird chemicals being added to beauty products, the consumer reports and recalls coming out daily, it makes it so hard to know what's safe to use and what's not. I'll totally admit that I have often found myself using hair products that have a bunch of ingredients I can't pronounce, like "paraphenylenediamine," for example. So as often as I can, I try to use items from my fridge or pantry in my beauty regiment in hopes of counteracting some of the crazy chemicals I've already subjected my hair and skin to. Hopefully, it will lower the risk of me growing a third arm or sixth finger. There are two masks I adore when it comes to my hair. I use these masks on both my natural hair and hair extensions.

> " *I try to use items from my fridge or pantry in my beauty regiment.*"

Conditioning Boost Mask: Honey, Eggs, Olive Oil, Conditioner

My mom actually introduced me to this mask during my teenaged years. The first time, I tried it on my own, I used way too many eggs and washed it out with scalding hot water. I was picking scrambled eggs out of my hair for hours. Don't make the same mistake I did. When you're washing it out, be sure to use cool water. I like this mask because it's like a supercharged version of your regular conditioner. I use OGX Renewing Moroccan Argon Oil Conditioner (which can be found at your local drugstore, Target, or Wal-Mart) as my base. It's great when it comes to moisturizing your hair. When it's combined with the yolk from the egg you get all the amazing nutrients like vitamin A (prevents breakage) and vitamin B12 (promotes hair growth). Not to mention the yolk gives your hair added shine while strengthening your hair follicles. Super win!

INGREDIENTS:

1 Egg (2 eggs for long hair)

3 Tablespoons Raw Honey

3 Tablespoons of Olive Oil

½ Cup of Moisturizing Hair Conditioner

DIRECTIONS:

Mix all the ingredients, including the conditioner, in a bowl. Apply to damp hair and comb through. Put a plastic cap over hair and let it set for 25-30 minutes. Rinse hair with cool water.

Deep Conditioning Yogurt + Honey Hair Mask

This mask is awesome for growing strong, healthy, soft hair. The lactic acid in the yogurt helps clear dead skin cells from your scalp and helps your follicles grow. The protein in yogurt also helps keep your hair strong and healthy. The honey not only makes your hair soft, but it helps attract and keep moisture locked into your hair.

INGREDIENTS:

¼ Cup Natural Yogurt

2 Tablespoons Raw Honey

½ Teaspoon Coconut Oil

DIRECTIONS:

Mix all the ingredients in a bowl (you might need to melt the coconut oil first if it's hard). Apply to damp hair and comb through. Put a plastic cap over hair and let it set for 20 minutes. Wash hair with your regular shampoo.

18. Favorite brands for hair dye

I've been wearing blue hair for almost a decade. I've pretty much tried just about every hair dye on the market. I've come across great brands and some pretty crappy ones as well. Presently, my three favorite brands of hair dye are:

1. Pravana – I love Pravana Blue because I get highlights, lowlights, and all kinds of vivid, iridescent color magic all in one tube. I don't have to mix various hues to end up with dimension. Typically to get this product you have to be a certified beautician and get it from a professional beauty supply store like Salon Centric, or Cosmo Pro. However, there are several providers on Amazon.com that you can order from without going through the hassle of obtaining your beautician's license.

2. Manic Panic – is easier to obtain. You can find it at Sally Beauty. With this brand, I typically mix two shades of blue to achieve the look I'm going for. The combination of 'Rockabilly Blue' and 'Shocking Blue' is one of my favorites.

3. Adore Hair Dye – is the most inexpensive of the three. This brand is sometimes harder to find at Sally Beauty and is more readily available at local beauty supply stores. With this brand, I mix 'Indigo Blue' and 'Baby Blue' to get the perfect summer blue hue.

19. Why Is My Hair Blue?

People give me way too much credit for being a pioneer of the blue hair movement. My hair is actually blue because of a freak accident that happened almost a decade ago. I went to my stylist requesting pink hair with purple highlights, and somehow I ended up with blue hair. Initially I was completely mortified. I even cried. I was so nervous and scared because I had never seen anybody wear blue hair, and thought I looked like a complete idiot. It wasn't a popular color. However, once I left the salon and made it to my next destination, I got a million compliments. Everyone loved my blue hair and were captivated (or so they told me) with the bold brown skin girl daring to wear blue hair. They had never seen anyone rock blue hair before. As a result of all the love I got on my new hued coif, I kept the color. I've been wearing blue since that day. And have never gone back to black.

20. How to dress while rocking colored hair without looking like a complete color-wheel disaster

As a girl who has been wearing blue hair for almost a decade, I definitely have had my fair share of experiences when it comes to dressing to complement my hair. Although I tend to go for blacks, black/white, and neutrals, I'm not scared to go for bold colors and fun prints.

1. *2.* *3.* *4.*

All in all, here's how I've learned over the years to dress for my hair.

1. One way to make colorful hues work is to use a monochromatic scheme to your advantage. For example, I'll take a color analogous to blue on the color-wheel and use it to craft majority of my outfit. Like my magenta suit look, for example.

2. …or you can take an opposite color on the color wheel and do the same thing. Like wearing yellow (since my hair is blue)

3. When playing with prints, I like to either choose prints in a complementary color or a related color. I've chosen a complementary color in red-based paisley print.

4. Here, I've chosen to go the analogous route with a plaid composed of blue and violet hues.

I like to have fun with my looks. Although there's a little bit of color science behind it all, I just go with what feels good. As long as you feel confident in it, other people are bound to pick up on your rad vibes; so do what works for you. Don't be afraid to experiment. And if all else fails, you can never go wrong with blacks, whites, and neutrals.

CHAPTER 4

Workout & Nutrition

> " Get comfortable with being uncomfortable."
>
> —Jillian Michaels

1. Favorite Workouts

Thanks to the Kim K.'s of the world, the latest body obsessions are to have a flat stomach, small waist, and a voluptuous backside. I too am on a quest to join the "What Waist?" tribe, so here are a few of my favorite exercises I do to keep my waist close to invisible and my butt close to "daaaaaayyyyuuumm" status.

Squat

Where It Works: Glutes, Hamstrings, Quads, Lower Back

Difficulty: Beginner/Intermediate

How To Do It: Stand up as erect and as tall as you can. Spread your feet shoulder-width apart and point your toes out slightly. Put your arms straight out in front of you. Lower your body as if you're about to take a seat. Go down as far as you can by pushing your hips back and bending your knees. Hold the position briefly, and then slowly push yourself back to the starting position in a controlled motion. Focus more on correct form and feeling the burn versus speed. When bending, it's super important to make sure your knees do not extend past your toes. Also be sure to keep your heels flat on the floor.

Glute Kickback

Where It Works: Glutes, Hamstrings

Difficulty: Beginner

How To Do It: Start on a mat with your palms and your knees on the floor. Your back should be parallel to the ground. In a controlled motion, without arching your back, Lift your right leg and thrust it backward. Your toes should be pointing downward toward the floor, and your leg should be extended. Focus on flexing your butt muscles before bringing the leg back down to your starting position. Repeat with your left leg to complete one repetition.

Back Lunges

Where It Works: Glutes, Hamstrings, Quads, Hip Flexors

Difficulty: Beginner/intermediate

How To Do It: Stand up as erect and as tall as you can with both feet together. Place your hands behind your neck just as you would if you were doing a sit-up. This will help you keep your balance. Using your right foot, take a step backwards and bend your knee when your right foot touches the ground. Keep lowering your body until your right knee almost touches the ground and the bend is almost at a 90-degree angle. In a controlled motion, raise yourself back up to the starting position. Repeat with your left leg to complete one repetition.

Static Plank

Where It Works: Core, Abdominals, Lower Back

Difficulty: Beginner/intermediate

How To Do It: Start by laying on a mat in a modified pushup position. Instead of resting with your palms to the floor as you would when doing a push up, you are going to bend your elbows 90 degrees and rest with both on your elbows and forearms on the floor. Your elbows should be directly underneath your shoulders, and you should be facing down toward the floor with your spine straight.

Once stable, squeeze your core by flexing your abs. It should feel as though you are trying to pull your belly button in towards your spine.

Once you are in position, hold the pose for 30 seconds to 1 minute. You will build up your endurance the more you do the exercise.

Side Plank

Where It Works: Oblique, Abdominals

Difficulty: Intermediate

How To Do It: Start by laying on a mat on your right side. Your right hip should be resting on the mat, and your legs should be extended. Place your right elbow directly under your shoulder and stabilize yourself by placing your forearm on the mat as well. Contract your abs and raise your hips from the mat. This should lift up your entire torso. Once you are in position, hold the pose for 30 seconds to 1-minute. You will build up your endurance the more you do the exercise.

22. How to stay motivated when it comes to working out

Every time I meet someone who says they enjoy working out; I either wonder what strange planet they are from or deem them to be a liar. The thought of someone actually enjoying the torture called physical exercise is beyond my comprehension. Nonetheless, physical activity is vital to living a healthy life. Plus, working out makes you look good naked. Who doesn't want to look good naked?

So what are some ways to get motivated to break a sweat?

> " *Who doesn't want to look good naked?* "

A FEW THINGS I LIKE TO DO:

- Make a "Body-Vision Board". It's very similar to a standard vision board; it's just body specific. I make a collage of images of bodies I admire; pictures of my goal weight; the healthy food I'd need to eat to get there; and I even post images of people working out. When I look at the board, it serves as a reminder of what I want and the work I need to put in to achieve the goals.

- Lurk fitness pages on social media. Looking at the perfectly defined abs of my favorite fitness gurus on Instagram makes me want to get up, get out, and get some of my own. It inspires me to see them going hard in the gym. Watching their progress gives me hope that my workout efforts are not in vain.

- Have an accountability partner. If you don't have a friend that wants to work out with you, or one that is determined to make fitness a part of their life, enlist your followers on social media. Some days when I don't want to work out, the only reason I go is because I know if I don't post a Snapchat story of myself in the gym, my followers are going to ask me why I didn't workout today. I made it a point to post on social media that I was trying to work out more because I knew I'd need them for motivation on the days I wasn't feeling it.

- Take progress photos. It's easy to not workout if you feel like you're not seeing results. Because results from working out are sometimes hard to see initially, I always take a photo on day 1, day 7, day 14, day 30, and so on. You'd be shocked to see how your body changes over time, and seeing those small milestones will encourage you to keep going.

- Switch up your routine occasionally to make workouts fun. Because I hate working out, I try to do things I know are more engaging and fun. Instead of running on a treadmill for hours, I go on hikes. It's much more stimulating for me to look at the scenery as I work my muscles, as opposed to staring at the clock and calorie count on a machine. I also enjoy boxing.

23. How to look cute while working out without doing the most

While we are not too far from the topic of how to stay motivated to work out, let's talk about fitness gear. Going shopping for cute athletic wear is definitely another way that I stay motivated to work out. Looking cute and feeling great definitely will get you going to the gym to bust a sweat. Although looking cute is the objective, we must also keep in mind that we are working out and not attending a runway show (i.e. – do not attempt to recreate the workout look in the illustration at the beginning of this chapter). Nothing baffles me more than seeing the girl at the gym with a face full of makeup, hair laid like she just came from the salon, and attire that looks like she's waiting to be called on stage at Magic City on a Monday.

When picking out workout clothes you should think about support, comfort, and style. Invest in some good sports bras. No one wants saggy boobs, and working out without the proper support garments can definitely cause just that.

You also want to make sure that your garments are breathable. The goal is to break a sweat. It's so important to buy clothes that are comprised of materials that will not irritate your skin and cause you discomfort.

Style is important too. Often, women starting on their fitness journey tend to be insecure with their bodies and will wear oversized, frumpy clothes to the gym to hide their problem areas. Wearing ill fitting or bigger clothing actually makes you look bigger, and mentally this makes you feel worse. You don't necessarily have to wear gym clothes made of spandex, but make sure that your clothes fit properly so you get a real sense of what your body looks like and how it's starting to change.

Nike sports bras and matching cycle shorts or leggings are always a go for me. They offer great support, they're comfortable, and super cute too. Nike makes so many fun patterns that you can wear them together or mix-and-match and have alternatives every time you go to workout. Not to mention that you can always throw a sweatshirt on or a light windbreaker on top and go to your next destination without looking too crazy.

Adidas is another one of my favorite places to get workout clothes. They have insanely cute matching sets.

We can't forget about sneakers. Finding a good pair of workout shoes is essential. Try to find a pair that go with the activity that you do the most. If you like to run, get a good running shoe. If you walk a lot, get a great walking shoe.

I always advise people who are buying new shoes to try shoes on in the middle of the day. In the middle of your day, your foot has swelled enough for you to properly assess how they'll feel when you are wearing them. Make sure the shoes you choose are comfortable.

24. *The thirst is real. The importance of staying hydrated while working out.*

Being thirsty is never a good thing; literally or figuratively. When your body starts sending you signals of thirst, you are already dehydrated. You should be drinking water throughout the day from the time you wake up to the time you go to bed. It's super important for you to drink more water when you're working out. Even if you don't sweat during the workout, your body is still losing water. Since our bodies are comprised of two-thirds water, and water is so vital to every function in our body, it's important to stay hydrated. Sports drinks like Gatorade and Powerade are awesome, but nothing beats H2O. If you are particular about the brand of water that you like, make sure you take your own water to the gym. If you forget your water, many gyms offer water fountains and some even have vending machines and juice bars. I get bored easily so I like to switch waters brands occasionally to fool my palate into thinking I'm drinking something new.

MY FAVORITE WATER BRANDS ARE:

Voss

Fiji

Boxed Water

Blk Premium Alkaline water

Dasani

...and Perrier Mineral Water with a lime wedge (for when I'm craving something fizzy and desperately trying to avoid a soda)

25. *My favorite cleanses*

When I say my favorite cleanses, I use the term loosely. I'm not going to deceive you into thinking there is anything pleasurable about a cleanse. They require a great deal of discipline, determination, and patience with those around you because you will be irritable.

Cleanses do have their high points though. They offer your body the opportunity to rid itself of toxins. Not to mention, you'll drop a good amount of weight if you stick with it. Who isn't down for a little weight loss?

The two cleanses I like to do are the "Master Cleanse" and a Juice Cleanse.

The first time I ever heard about the "Master Cleanse" was when I was in high school, and my mom told us she would be drinking only lemonade for the next 10 days and for us to try not to annoy the living daylights out of her. I will admit that I didn't actually get into it until years later when I saw an article about it being one of Beyonce's go-to's when she wants to drop weight quickly. This cleanse is super insane and not for the faint of heart. You basically drink a semi spicy, lemonade-like concoction, and herbal detox tea for 10 days straight. No food at all - just the lemonade, tea, and water. If you're bold enough to embark on the journey, here's the recipe:

Master Cleanse Recipe

INGREDIENTS:

Two Tablespoons of organic lemon Juice (use fresh lemon, not lemon juice in a can or squeeze-bottle)

Two Tablespoons of Organic grade B maple syrup (not the commercial, grade-A maple syrup you use for breakfast)

$\frac{1}{10}$ Teaspoon Cayenne pepper

Ten ounces of filtered water

DIRECTIONS:

Combine all the ingredients, mix thoroughly and enjoy.

Makes one serving

KEYS TO THIS DETOX:

Drink a minimum of 6 to 12 glasses throughout the day whenever you are hungry

Drink an herbal laxative tea every night. (I drink "Smooth Moves")

Optional: If you want, you can also do a salt flush every morning. It tastes absolutely disgusting in my opinion, but it totally makes you go to the bathroom, and eliminating waste is always good.

Saltwater Flush Recipe

2 Teaspoons of Sea Salt

1 Liter of Pure Water

Drink this salt flush on an empty stomach 2-3 hours before you leave the house in the morning. The last place you want to be when this stuff kicks in is away from an unfamiliar toilet. (*You will most likely have 1-2 bowel movements with each salt flush.)

Also make sure to drink the entire salt flush in one sitting. Try to drink it in 5 minutes or less. If you pace it any longer than this, it might not work.

Stay focused. This detox is tougher on the mind than it is the body. If you stay strong, you'll feel so accomplished at the end.

> " *If you stay strong, you'll feel so accomplished at the end.*"

Juicing

The second type of cleanse I do is a juice cleanse. I love eating, and I find legitimate pleasure in food so no liquid based cleanse is enjoyable for me. But, a juice cleanse is a lot easier for me than the master cleanse. With a juice cleanse you get more variety in the beverages you're consuming. Plus, if you get too hungry and need to chew to feel satisfied, you can always eat the raw vegetables in your juice without feeling too bad or like you've fallen off the wagon. When you're juicing, it's totally ok to eat a green apple, or some carrots, or kale. Just make sure you're only eating the raw vegetables and fruit. Don't add salad dressing or anything else. I have a juicer and make my own juice sometimes. However, a lot of times I'm ridiculously busy and just don't have the time it takes to prep and make my own juices. Instead, I order from any cold-pressed juicer in the city I'm in. Many of them have "cleanse programs" where they have the different juices selected for you and they tell you how frequently and the order in which you should drink them. It makes it so easy to stay on track and destroys the excuse, "I don't have time." Simply grab a cooler and your juices and hit the road.

26. Favorite Places To Grab A Cold-Pressed Juice

Atlanta

DTOX BUCKHEAD
http://dtoxjuice.com/
3210 Roswell Road Atlanta, GA 30305

ARDENS GARDENS
http://www.ardensgarden.com/
3757 Roswell Rd NE Atlanta, GA 30342

Charlotte

VIVA RAW
https://viva-raw.com
224 E 7th St, Charlotte, NC 28202

Chicago

PEELED JUICE BAR
http://peeledjuicebar.com
1571 Sheffield Avenue Chicago, IL 60614

Dallas

THE GEM
http://www.insidethegem.com/
6030 Luther Lane, Suite 160 Dallas, TX 75225

Houston

FLOW JUICE BAR
http://www.flowjuicebar.com
214 Fairview St, Houston, TX 77006

Los Angeles

Pressed Juicery
pressedjuicery.com
6201 Hollywood Blvd #128 Los Angeles, CA 90028

New York

Liquiteria
liquiteria.com
170 Second Avenue (Corner of 2nd Ave. and 11th St.) New York, NY 10003

Pittsburgh

The Pittsburgh Juice Company
pittsburghjuicecompany.com
3418 Penn Avenue, Pittsburgh PA 15201

Phoenix

Kaleidoscope Juice
kaleidoscopejuice.com
1 N 1st St. Phoenix, AZ 85004

San Francisco

Pressed Juicery
pressedjuicery.com
2162A Union Street San Francisco, CA 94123

27. Thirty Day Ultimate Fat Burn Meal Plan

My good friends at Hybrid Impact Fitness have agreed to let me share their super coveted 30-day meal plan. This meal plan is no joke. However, it got my waistline the smallest it's ever been. Not to mention I felt super healthy and had a ton of energy. The plan is designed to prepare your body for the ultimate fat burn:

Week 1: For Best Results Do the 3day Detox

Day 1 – Day 3: Complete The Three-Day Super-Food Detox Regimen

Day 1 (of 3Day Detox)
Breakfast: Kale & spinach smoothie (juice one cucumber, one sweet red apple.) Add the juice to blender. Add 4 – 5 kale leaves and handful of spinach and blend. If you want it "extra green" add more kale.

* If you don't have a blender to make smoothies you can simply make a kale & spinach salad with cucumber and red apple. This is an alternative, so there's no excuse not to remain consistent.

Snack: one bowl fruit salad (peaches, strawberries, blueberries. Sprinkle with a little lemon or lime juice)

Lunch: 1 cup brown rice or 1cup quinoa, 1 cup sautéed squash & zucchini w/ onions & garlic, ½ cup Black beans

Snack: two Handfuls of nuts (almonds or walnuts)

Dinner: 1 cup brown rice or 1 cup quinoa, 1 cup steamed carrots & parsnips (sliced or julienne cut), spinach & strawberry salad (drizzle lemon or lime juice on for dressing)

DAY TWO (OF 3DAY DETOX)

Breakfast: Kale & spinach smoothie (juice one cucumber, one sweet red apple.) Add the juice to blender. Add 4 – 5 kale leaves and handful of spinach and blend. If you want it "extra green" then just add more kale.

* If you don't have a blender to make smoothies you can simply make a kale & spinach salad with cucumber and red apple. This is an alternative, so there's no excuse not to remain consistent.

Snack: 1 bowl fruit salad (papaya, peaches, nectarines) add raw or roasted walnuts

Lunch: 1 cup Wild Rice or 1 cup quinoa, 1 cup Brussels sprouts, ½ cup choice of black beans, red beans or adzuki beans

Snack: 1 bowl of fruit (choose from pineapple, watermelon, dark red or purple grapes)

Dinner: 1 cup Quinoa or 1 cup Wild Rice, 1 cup steamed Brussels Sprouts, ½ cup Choice of Black beans, Red beans or Adzuki beans

DAY 3 (OF 3DAY DETOX)

Breakfast: Kale & spinach smoothie (juice one cucumber, one sweet red apple.) Add the juice to blender. Add 4 – 5 kale leaves and handful of spinach and blend. If you want it "extra green" then just add more kale.

* If you don't have a blender to make smoothies you can simply make a kale & spinach salad with cucumber and red apple. This is an alternative, so there's no excuse not to remain consistent.

Snack: 2 Handfuls of nuts (almonds or walnuts)

Lunch: 1 cup brown rice, 2 cups sliced red pepper, yellow peppers, onions, garlic sautéed together, 1⁄2 cup black beans

Snack: 1 bowl fruit salad (papaya, peaches, nectarines) add raw or roasted walnuts

Dinner: 1 cup quinoa, 1 cup steamed carrots & parsnips (sliced or julienne cut), spinach & strawberry salad (drizzle lemon or lime juice on for dressing)

DAYS 4 – DAY 7: CHICKEN BREAST & TUNA AS YOUR LEAN PROTEIN

Breakfast: Lean Protein & complex carb—egg whites scrambled and 1/2 cup oatmeal or 3 slices of turkey bacon, 2 hard boiled eggs (remove yolk) and 1/2 grapefruit

Drink a 20 oz bottle of water with meal.

Mid-Morning Snack: Lean Protein & Fruit—2oz tuna packet & 1/2 Grapefruit or 1 cup of almonds or walnuts and 1 orange.

Drink a 20 oz bottle of water with meal.

Lunch: Lean protein, complex carb & vegetable—3oz chicken breast, 1/2 med sweet potato, 1 cup greens or steamed veggies or chicken Salad, & 1 apple.

Drink a 20 oz bottle of water with meal.

Mid-Afternoon Snack: Lean protein & fruit—3oz chicken breast & 1/4 cup cantaloupe or fat free yogurt and 1cup of mixed berry fruit

Dinner: Lean protein, complex carb & vegetable—3 oz baked chicken breast, small sweet potato & 1-2 cups of steamed veggies or grilled chicken in a high fiber, low carb wheat wrap & 1 cup of steamed veggies.

Drink a 20 oz bottle of water with meal.

PM Snack (optional): Lean protein & fruit—2 oz tuna pack & 1/2 cup mixed berries

Week 2: Fish & protein shake as your lean protein for week

Breakfast: Complex carb & fruit—2 cup oatmeal w/ apple slices , three hard boiled eggs (remove yolk) and 1cup of mixed fruit.

Drink a 20 oz bottle of water with meal.

Mid-Morning Snack: Protein shake—15-20 grams of protein per serving. Add fresh or frozen fruit of choice or 1 cup of fat free yogurt and 1 cup of mixed fruit.

Lunch: Lean protein, complex carb & vegetable—herb encrusted red snapper, small sweet potato & green salad or baked salmon over a spinach salad.

Drink a 20 oz bottle of water with meal.

Mid-Afternoon Snack: Protein shake—15-20 grams of protein per serving. Add fresh or frozen fruit of choice. Or one large orange and Fiber one bar.

Dinner: Lean protein, complex carb & vegetable—baked tilapia with 1 cup quinoa & Kale Salad OR Baked salmon, 1 cup wild rice & spinach salad

Drink a 20 oz bottle of water with meal.

PM Snack (optional): Mixed Berries or 1 Grapefruit

Week 3: Turkey breast & tuna as your lean protein

Breakfast: Lean protein & fruit—4 strips of turkey bacon low sodium & 1⁄2 cup of Mixed Berries or 3 egg whites scrambled in a High Fiber, Low carb whole-wheat wrap

Drink a 20 oz bottle of water with meal.

Mid-Morning Snack: Lean protein & vegetables—3oz Tuna pack & 1 cup greens or 1 cup or almonds or walnuts and grape fruit

Lunch: Lean protein, complex carb & vegetables—3 oz Turkey breast, 1⁄2 cup brown rice & 1 cup mixed veggies or Ground turkey patty in a high Fiber, low carb wheat wrap & 1 cup of mixed veggies

Drink a 20 oz bottle of water with meal.

Mid-Afternoon Snack: Lean protein, & vegetables—3oz fresh tuna & 1 cup greens.

Dinner: Lean protein, complex carb & vegetables—3 oz turkey breast, 1⁄2 cup quinoa & 1 cup mixed veggies or baked turkey wings, mixed veggies and small salad.

Drink a 20 oz bottle of water with meal.

PM Snack (optional): fruit—for example, 1⁄2 grapefruit or 1⁄2 cup mixed berries.

Week 4: Mix it up a little... choose either fish, poultry, or turkey

Breakfast: two egg whites & 1⁄2 cup cooked oatmeal, 1⁄2 cup mixed berries or fat free yogurt & one grapefruit.

Drink a 20 oz bottle of water with meal.

Mid-Morning Snack: Protein shake—15-20 grams of protein per serving add fresh or frozen fruit of choice. Or kale & spinach smoothie from detox

Lunch: Lean protein, complex carb & green vegetables—chicken salad with side of mixed fruit or 4oz pack of tuna, side salad and 1 piece of fruit

Drink a 20 oz bottle of water with meal.

Mid-Afternoon Snack: fat free yogurt and fiber one bar

Dinner: Lean protein, complex carb, leafy greens—baked salmon, mixed green veggies, and 1⁄2 cup wild rice or 4oz sirloin, sweet potato and mixed veggies

Drink a 20 oz bottle of water with meal.

PM Snack (Optional): Mixed berries

Water Water Water Water Water and More Water—cut out the Soda, Sugary Juices and Caffeine.

Remember to cook all meats and chop up all veggies on Saturday or Sunday as a meal preparation day in order to be prepared for the week.

CHAPTER 5

SWANK Eats

> 66 I'm just someone who likes cooking and for whom sharing food is a form of expression."
> —Maya Angelou

28. Basic things every woman should have in her kitchen.

If you plan on cooking (or even pretending to cook, LOL) there are a few basic cooking utensils and appliances you should have in your kitchen. You don't have to necessarily spend a million bucks on utensils and appliances, but in this area I like to invest in quality items so I don't have to keep replacing them constantly.

APPLIANCES:

-Microwave

-Blender

-Toaster

*OPTIONAL APPLIANCES:

-Juicer: This one should only be purchased if you plan on making juice cleanses a part of your life and want to save money in the long run by making your own juices versus buying cold-pressed juices.

-Kuerig (or coffee maker)

Tools & Utensils

-Glass Chopping Board

-Can Opener

-Corkscrew

-Bottle Opener

-Cheese Grater

-Garlic Press

-Knife Block Set that includes: Kitchen Shears, 8" Carving Knife, 8" Chef Knife, 8" Bread Knife, 7" Santoku Knife, 6" Boning Knife, 5" Utility Knife, 3" Paring Knife, and 6- 4 ½ " Steak Knives

-Whisk

-Spatula

-Slotted Turner

-Stirring Spoon

-Slotted Spoon

-Ladle

-Tongs

-Meat Fork

-Measuring Cups

-Measuring Spoons

-Mixing Bowls (of various sizes)

-Colander

-Set of pots and pans that include: 1-qt. covered saucepan, 2-qt. covered saucepan, 8-qt. covered stockpot, 3-qt. covered sauté pan, 8.5" frying pan, 10" frying pan

- Cookie sheet

-9*9 inch baking pan

-Muffin pan

29. How To Set A Table

Let's keep it real here, how often have you been placed in front of a table with a bunch of forks and a bunch of spoons and cringed a little at the thought of using the wrong fork for the wrong course? Well, I'm here to save the day. Here's a guide to set a table properly.

Your dinner plate (F.) should always be placed in the center. You can place it atop a charger (G.) for formal settings. If you're serving soup, a soup bowl (E.) goes on top of the dinner plate. Everything else on the table will be placed around this plate. Be advised that flatware is arranged in the order it will be used. So if you're ever in a fancy restaurant and you're in doubt of which fork or spoon to use, use the one furthest away from the dinner plate. Forks go to the left of the plate. The dinner fork (B.) is placed to the immediate left of the plate. The salad fork (A.) is placed to the left of the dinner fork. If you're not serving salad, it's ok to eliminate this fork all together. Dessert forks are typically brought out when dessert is served. However, if you really want it on the table during the meal, it's ok to place it between the dinner plate and the dinner fork. Spoons and knives go to the right of the dinner plate. The knife (H.) should be placed to the immediate right of the dinner plate, and the beverage spoon (I.) should be placed to the right of

the knife. The soup spoon (J.) is then placed to the right of the beverage spoon. Or you can bring the spoon out when the soup is being served. The same applies with a dessert spoon. You can bring it out when dessert is being served, or place it to the right of the soup spoon.

Place the bread plate (or salad plate) (C.) to the left of the dinner plate directly above the forks. The butter knife (D.) goes on top of the bread plate. The drinking glasses are to be placed to the right of the dinner plate above the knife and spoons. The glasses to include in your setting depend on what beverages you're serving. You should place a coffee cup (L.) and saucer (K.) directly above the knife and spoons. The water glass (M.) should be placed to the left of the coffee cup. Wine glasses (N., O.,) are to be placed to the left of the water glass.

> ❝ *Let's keep it real here.*❞

30. How to be a good dinner host

For me, being a good dinner host boils down to preparation and presentation. The two go hand in hand.

The first thing you want to do is determine your theme and guest list. Do you want a fun fiesta-themed dinner with your favorite couples, or a Sex-and-the-City inspired dinner with your closest girlfriends? It's important to decide this early so you can curate a menu that's aligned with what you're going for. What you decide to serve to a dinner party of six of your closest girlfriends will be significantly different from what you decide to serve for a sexy dinner between you and your significant other.

Picking a theme and narrowing down your guests will also help you decide what type of invites you want to send, the music you want to play, and the type of décor you want to use in your house for your table-setting that day.

Once you've determined the vibe of your shindig, you want to send invites. Personally, I like to mail out hand-written (or custom) invitations. It goes the extra mile and adds a touch of class in an era where everything is so hurried and instant. In addition to snail-mail invites, I sometimes send email invitations. The one thing I rarely do is call to invite because I never want to put my guests on the spot. I'd much rather they are able to take their time, weigh their options, determine if they can attend, and get back to me. Which is why it's important to request an RSVP on either your hand-written invites or email. You need to know who to expect so you can plan and shop for food accordingly.

In your preparation stage make sure you list any décor items you might need to set the theme. It's cute to go the extra mile by making place cards for your guests. If you choose to do place cards, you need to make these in advance as well. I also like to make playlists in advance too so I'm not worried about music on the day of the event. You're going to have a bunch of stuff to juggle that day so the last thing you want to worry about is what song to play next.

Also, determine what you want to serve and make a grocery list of the items you need to pick up. It's best to go grocery shopping the day before (unless you plan on serving something that needs to be super fresh, like lobster – which you should pick up the morning of). I also like to pick out my outfit the day before as well.

A few hours before the dinner (about 4-5 hours before) I do all the prep-work required for the dinner. I cut the vegetables, clean and season the meat, chill the wine, set the table, etc. I make it so all I have to do an hour before the dinner is take things out of the fridge and throw them in the oven (or in a pot).

About 3 hours before dinner, I shower, and do my hair, and makeup. I like to take my time on my hair and makeup so I would much rather do it well before my guests arrive than to keep them waiting because I'm trying to glue an eyelash on last minute.

Once my hair and makeup are done, I go back to the kitchen and begin cooking. Although, I do my hair and makeup in advance, I don't put on my outfit until about 10-15 minutes before the guests are scheduled to arrive. God forbid I spill something on it while cooking. It's important to begin cooking closer to when your guests arrive (versus earlier in the day) so the food can be hot and fresh. I hate reheating food. I like my guests to get it fresh out of the oven or off the stove.

When your guests arrive, be sure to greet them. Offer your guests a beverage (water, wine, cocktail, etc.) and hors d'oeuvres before you seat them in the living room or lounge area. I wait until all the guests are present before escorting them collectively to the dinner table. It's awkward and a tad bit rude to seat guests at the table while you wait on other guests to arrive. Try to seat everyone at the same time.

Once seated, make sure you're sitting at the head of the table. If you have a spouse or significant other in attendance, seat them at the opposing end from you.

Try not to seat one of your guests at the end of the table so they're not forced to feel as though they need to host or entertain in any way.

Keep dinner conversations light, and fun. Constantly check on your guests and refill any beverages if need be. You should tend to your guests just as a wait staff would tend to you if you were dining in a restaurant. Unless you're super fancy and have hired wait staff for the evening, you're your guests' waitress.

> " *Being a good dinner host boils down to preparation and presentation.*"

31. A Few Of My Favorite Recipes:

Lobster/Shrimp Macaroni & Cheese

INGREDIENTS:

16 Ounces of Medium Shells or Elbow Macaroni

Olive Oil

Sea Salt

1 Quart milk

8 Tablespoons unsalted butter, divided

½ Cup all-purpose flour

12 Ounces Gruyere cheese, (grated)

8 Ounces extra-sharp Cheddar, (grated)

½ Teaspoon ground black pepper

½ Teaspoon nutmeg

4 Lobster Tails, (cooked)

½ Pound Shrimp, (cooked)

1 ½ cups bread crumbs

* Serves 6

DIRECTIONS:

Preheat oven to 375 degrees Fahrenheit

Bring a large pot of water to a boil. Add 2TBS of Olive Oil, Salt, and Pasta to the pot. Cook the pasta according to the directions on the package. Once done, drain pasta and set aside.

While the pasta is cooking, chop the lobster meat and shrimp into desired size.

In a small saucepan, heat the milk until it's warm, but NOT boiling.

In a separate large pot, melt 6TBS of butter. Whisk in the flour to create a roux. Let the roux cook on low heat for 1-2 minutes, then slowly add the warm milk. Cook for another 1-2 minutes. Make sure you whisk the mixture continuously during this time.

Turn off the heat, then add the Cheddar Cheese, Gruyere Cheese, 1TBS salt, pepper, and nutmeg. Mix thoroughly.

Then add the pasta, lobster meat and shrimp, and stir well

Place mixture in baking dish

Melt 2TBS of butter, and mix with the bread crumbs, and then sprinkle on the top of the mixture.

Bake for 30 to 35 minutes at 375 degrees Fahrenheit. The macaroni will be browned on top and the sauce bubbly once it's done.

ENJOY!

Herb Crusted Salmon Recipe

Ingredients:

4 (5-Ounce) salmon fillets

5 Tablespoons fresh lemon juice, divided

¾ Teaspoon lemon pepper seasoning

1 Teaspoon parsley

1 Teaspoon dried thyme

10 Tablespoons butter, divided

1 Shallot, minced

1 Tablespoon white wine vinegar

¼ Cup white wine

1 Cup heavy cream

* Serves 4

Directions:

Rub salmon with 3 Tablespoons lemon juice. Season the non-skin side with lemon pepper, parsley, thyme. Set aside.

Heat 2 Tablespoons butter over medium heat in a pan, and sauté shallot for 2 minutes until tender. Mix in remaining 2 Tablespoons lemon juice, vinegar, and ¼ cup wine. Simmer until reduced by at least ½ .

Stir in heavy cream. Season sauce with salt, and white pepper to taste. Cook and stir until thickened. Whisk in 4 Tablespoons butter. Set aside and keep warm.

Heat remaining 4 Tablespoons butter in a skillet over medium heat. Place salmon in the skillet herb side down, and cook 1 to 2 minutes, until seared. Remove salmon and set aside herb side up. Put salmon in the skillet with the sauce. Make sure salmon is herb side up, and cook 8 minutes in the sauce, or until easily flaked with a fork.

Serve salmon on plate with sauce, paired with steamed asparagus, and mashed red potatoes.

Red Wine Braised Short Ribs

INGREDIENTS:

5 Pounds bone-in beef short ribs

1 Pound bag of Baby Carrots

2 Medium white onions, chopped

4 Celery stalks, chopped

6 garlic cloves, halved

1 750 ml bottle of Cabernet Sauvignon

2 Cups Beef stock

½ Cup vegetable oil

½ Cup all-purpose flour, divided

1 Tablespoon tomato paste

1/3 Cup parsley, chopped

3 Bay leaves

2 Tablespoon thyme

1 Tablespoon oregano

1 Tablespoon rosemary

Sea salt

Ground black pepper

Serves 4

DIRECTIONS:

Preheat oven to 350° Fahrenheit.

Season short ribs with salt and pepper, and then coat them in flour.

Heat oil in a large Dutch oven over medium-high heat and brown short ribs on all sides, about 2 minutes on each side. Once browned, remove ribs from pot and set aside.

Scrape out any residue from pot leaving a small amount of oil behind.

Add carrots, onions, and celery to the pot and cook over medium-high heat for about 3-4 minutes

Add red wine, 3 tablespoons of flour, and tomato paste. Mix well and let simmer for 3 minutes.

Then add short ribs and bring to a boil. Once boiling, reduce the heat to medium and cook for 30 minutes. The liquid should reduce by half.

Add beef stock, garlic, parsley, bay leaves, thyme, oregano and Rosemary to the pot. Bring to a boil.

Season with more salt and pepper then transfer pot to the oven. Bake for 2 hours at 350 degrees Fahrenheit.

Serve ribs on top of mashed potatoes with vegetables plated on the side.

32. Know Your Glassware

Different libations call for different glasses. No matter the alcoholic beverage you choose, you want to make sure you have the appropriate vessel to serve it in. Here's a crash course in glassware.

BEVERAGE: BEER

GLASSWARE SERVED IN: PINT GLASS

What & Why: There are two standard types of pint glasses. The Imperial/British pint glass is 20 ounces, while the American pint is only 16 ounces. Most pint glasses you'll see in a bar are a simple, cylinder shape that widens as you approach the top. (Although it's not uncommon to come across jug-like pint glasses with a handle)

BEVERAGE: COGNAC

GLASSWARE SERVED IN: BRANDY SNIFTER

What & Why: A brandy snifter is a pretty sophisticated, pear-shaped glass with a wide body and narrow opening. The short-stem and wide bottom are perfect for cupping the glass in your hand to warm the liquor and release the aroma.

BEVERAGE: MARTINI

GLASSWARE SERVED IN: MARTINI GLASS

What & Why: I was first introduced to a martini glass when Carrie ordered a 'Cosmopolitan' on Sex and the City. The drink looked so sexy and high-class. Little did I know then that the cone-shape of the martini glass is really to prevent the different ingredients in your martini from separating.

BEVERAGE: ANY CARBONATED COCKTAIL

GLASSWARE SERVED IN: HIGHBALL GLASS

What & Why: The highball glass holds about 8 to 12 fluid ounces and is taller than your typical old-fashioned glass. The highball is great for any mixed drink containing a carbonated beverage because it's built to keep your beverage less exposed to air, causing it to stay carbonated longer. Nobody wants a flat drink, so if it has soda of any kind in it, go with a highball glass.

BEVERAGE: ANYTHING "ON THE ROCKS"

GLASSWARE SERVED IN: LOWBALL GLASS

What & Why: Lowball glasses are amongst the shorter, wider glasses of the glassware family. They're best for serving drinks requested 'on the rocks' because they tend to hold less liquid, making them ideal for holding a few shots of liquor

BEVERAGE: WHITE WINE

GLASSWARE SERVED IN: WHITE WINE GLASS

What & Why: White wine is typically served chilled in a slimmer wine glass because the smaller glass slows down any rise in temperature. This is another glass you should hold by the stem as not to heat the vino up indirectly with your hands.

BEVERAGE: RED WINE

GLASSWARE SERVED IN: RED WINE GLASS

What & Why: Compared to white wine, red wine is served in a wider, more bowl-shaped glass to release more of the aroma

BEVERAGE: CHAMPAGNE

GLASSWARE SERVED IN: FLUTE

What & Why: Champagne should always be served in a flute. The small surface area helps the beverage stay carbonated longer. Not to mention flutes are more aesthetically pleasing because they are better for showing off the bubbles that rise to the top of the glass.

> " *No matter the alcoholic beverage you choose, you want to make sure you have the appropriate vessel to serve it in.* "

33. MIXOLOGY 101: A Few of my Favorite Cocktail Recipes

Moscow Mule

INGREDIENTS:

1 half lime

2 ounces vodka

4 to 6 ounces ginger beer (my favorite brand to use is: Cock'n Bull)

DIRECTIONS:
Squeeze lime into a copper mug. Add three large ice cubes. Add vodka. Fill with cold ginger beer. Stir gently. Garnish with lime wedge.

*Makes 1 drink

SWANK's Electric Lemonade

INGREDIENTS:

1 ½ ounces vodka (I prefer peach Ciroc)

6 to 8 ounces of your favorite lemonade   (I prefer 'Simply Lemonade')

Splash of ginger ale

2 Lemon slices and 3 raspberries for garnish

DIRECTIONS
Fill a previously frozen mason jar with ice. Add vodka and top with lemonade. Shake until vodka and lemonade are mixed. Add a splash of ginger ale. Garnish with raspberries and lemon slices.

*Makes 1 drink

Beautiful One

INGREDIENTS:

1 ½ ounce Grand Marnier

1 ½ ounce Hennessy

2 ounces cranberry juice

2 Maraschino cherries

DIRECTIONS:

Fill a lowball glass with ice. Pour in Grand Marnier and Hennessy. Add cranberry juice. Stir. Garnish with speared cherries.

*Makes 1 drink

CHAPTER 6

Friendships

> ❝ It's important to make friendships that are deeper than gossiping and drinking and smoking and going out. Make friends who you can go get breakfast with, make friends you can cry with, make friends who support your life goals and believe in you."
>
> —*Unknown*

> **" *It's so much easier to maintain a healthy friendship when you are friends with the right people.* "**

34. Ask Olori: How do you manage to maintain friendships in such a catty industry?

I think the answer lies more so in the types of people you become friends with. It's so much easier to maintain a healthy friendship when you are friends with the right people. When it comes to my friends, I choose them very wisely and carefully. If I get a bad vibe from someone immediately, I follow my gut and do not proceed with cultivating a friendship. Don't get me wrong, I'm not mean, rude, or standoffish to them. I am always polite, courteous, and cordial; I'm just not buddy-buddy. I won't be on the phone with them having woe-is-me conversations at 5am, and I'm definitely not inviting them to my house to chill. The people that I call friends are like-minded, focused, and have extremely positive attitudes.

They inspire me and I in turn inspire them. The relationship is always mutually beneficial. It never feels one-sided or sketchy. Oprah once said, "You can't be friends with someone who wants your life." This is so true. If they are constantly trying to be you, or compete with you, that's a red flag, this is not a healthy friendship. Find friends that are satisfied with being themselves and that have their own lives and you can't go wrong. ...but if a friend you thought was good goes bad, read section 39!

35. The six types of friends every woman needs in her life

My mother always told me to watch the company that I keep. One bad apple will spoil the bunch. I am so particular about my friends, because I know that whether I know it or not their good and bad habits are rubbing off on me. I don't allow negative people in my space, and I don't do the gossip thing either. Everyone I allow in my life has to add some sense of value and purpose. When my friends and I have girl talk, we are talking about things like new listings for commercial real estate properties, a great new accountant we just discovered, the latest must-try restaurant for sushi, etc. We are never negatively discussing or bashing other people. You gain absolutely nothing from doing that and involving yourself with people who like to do such things. Eleanor Roosevelt said it best when she said, "Great minds discuss ideas; average minds discuss events; small minds discuss people." Be as picky about who you hang out with as you are your weave. That being said, these are the six types of friends I encourage you to add to your clique.

I. "You Go, Girl" Friend

Life is hard and sometimes you're going to feel like it sucks. You're going to get down on yourself, and want to throw a pity party. The "You Go, Girl" friend is super positive and always there to offer up a word of encouragement. She helps you to not dwell on your misfortunes, but encourages you to focus on the blessings to come. Whenever you're absolutely feeling like crap, this is the friend you call to bring you back to the light. She reminds you of how awesome you are when you forget. Think of her as the captain of your cheer squad.

II. "Girl, Bye" Friend

My "Girl, Bye" friend is the one who is always going to keep it real with me no matter how successful I get or how important I feel. She's always there to bring me right back to earth when I'm feeling myself and I'm about to make a really bad decision. Whether it be shaving half my head off in the shape of a lightning bolt, or deciding to drag a troll on social media, she's the friend to talk me out of it. Just as rational as she is blunt, this isn't the friend that sugarcoats anything. She tells you like it is, and forces you to deal. We all need this friend in our life, to keep us out of trouble and to keep us from waking up tomorrow regretting what we did last night.

III. "Ride, or Die" Friend

Your "Ride, or Die" friend is just as the name suggests, she's down for whatever. Want to roll past your boyfriend's house at 2am because he's not answering the phone (don't do this by the way)? She's down. Want to take an impromptu trip to Cabo? She's down. Want to open a bakery that only sells exotic flavored cupcakes? She's down to help wherever you need her. You might even consider this friend a best friend or sister. You never have to question where her loyalty lies. She's in it for the long haul. Never get rid of this friend. She most likely knows all your secrets.

IV. "The Smarter Friend"

It's very important to have a friend that is more knowledgeable than you. I've always heard if you are the smartest person in the room then you are in the wrong room. This friend is the friend that is always teaching you something and making you better at something whether intentionally or not. When you're in a bind and need to figure something out, this is the person you call. They are your favorite brain to pick.

> " *Everyone I allow in my life has to add some sense of value and purpose.*"

V. "The Business Bestie"

If you're in business for yourself, you are going to want to have someone who also owns a business that you can share resources with and listen to each other and be a source of encouragement. Entrepreneurship is far from easy. Every entrepreneur needs someone that has his or her back along the way, and this person is it for you. Since this person owns a business, they know and understand and can sympathize with some of the issues that only other entrepreneurs can understand. You can vent to this person about your business woes and you will not get strange and confusing responses back from them. They get it because they've been there. You can bounce ideas off one another and ultimately this person is a strong support system to you during the building/growth of your business.

VI. "The Sophisti-ratchet" Friend

You're going to work hard in your daily life and you're going to want to play harder. This is the friend that you hit the scene with. You and this friend share many social interests. They're not too professional/rigid and not too wild either. They know how to act and adapt in any environment. You can go with them to the opera or the strip club alike and they know how to operate in either place. They are the perfect blend of sophistication and ratchetness.

VS

> ❝ *You are a product of the five people you hang around the most.*❞

36. Boundaries: Drawing the line between friendship and business

A lot of people have heard the adage, "you are a product of the five people you hang around the most." Most successful people live by this. The more successful you become, the more likely you are to hang around equally, if not more, successful people. Although we are often lead to believe that many major deals are secured through submitting proposals and setting up meetings, a lot of meetings actually happen by chance gatherings between friends. So how do you make sure that you keep the boundary lines between friendship and business unblurred? It can become very hard to separate the lines depending on how close you become. So many of my friends are uber successful, and casual conversations quickly turn into lucrative business ideas. So how is it that you set these plans into motion without maybe ruining a friendship in the future? I have a few rules that I live by when it comes to doing business with friends.

"HAVE YOUR PEOPLE CALL THEIR PEOPLE"

This one is one of my favorites. Early in my career I used to be so nervous to talk about money. I was even more nervous to talk about money and deals with friends. I was always nervous that I might offend someone with my rate, or that I might give myself the short end of the stick by trying to be "nice" and likable. What makes this rule really great for me is that by passing off the baton to my team/representative, someone else is doing the negotiating.

I don't have to worry about my friend getting offended by any of my terms during the negotiation process. And if my friend doesn't like the terms, they won't have to feel like they are personally offending me by telling me that those terms are not acceptable to them. Even though it seems like your friend would be offended if you told your people to call their people or vice versa, the opposite is actually quite true. If your friend is successful, they will definitely have a team conducting business on their behalf. This team could include their manager, lawyer, advisor, and/or business partners. By suggesting that your team contact their team, you're actually taking some of the strain off of your friendship and some of the pressure that successful people face when juggling business and personal. Most likely your friend will appreciate you wanting to follow their standard protocol and not do "homie business." Every successful friend admires professionalism. I'm at a point where even if I come up with a good idea that I want my successful friend involved in, I'm more likely to reach out to their management before I even reach out to them personally. I never want to put them on the spot or make them feel obligated. I am respectful of their business choices, and as a businessperson myself I understand that every proposition isn't beneficial to everyone. Just because I think it's a good idea doesn't mean that it's going to fit into my friend's business model. Approaching their representative with the idea first, helps my friend to make smart decisions for them. Thereby making me an even better friend. This is what I do to my friends personally, and they love me for it

"Respect your friend's rates"

You, more than anyone else, should know the value of your friend's worth. Don't cheapen your respect for them, by trying to lowball them because you know you can get away with it. Whenever hiring my friend for a service, I always ask them for their "real "rate. I want them to know that I am willing to pay for the full price of their services, because they are worth it. Most likely your friend will tell you their real rate but also tell you that they don't feel comfortable charging you that because you are a friend. This is OK, and actually quite expected. It's OK to pay them what they ask you to pay. Just make sure you at least let them know you are willing to pay full price as you value and appreciate their unique ability. Let them offer you the discount; never ask for it. Most likely they'll give you a discount anyway.

"FOLLOW UP AND FOLLOW THROUGH"

Just because they are your friend doesn't mean that they deserve your excuses. When doing business with friends, don't get comfortable. Make sure you treat them like how you would treat your most important client. Don't think you can be late on deadlines, or be lackadaisical in your work thinking that they will "understand." It's not fair to your friends to have to deal with your BS simply because they are your friends. If you wouldn't do it to Rihanna, don't do it to your friend. Let your word be your bond. If you say you'll deliver by the third, wow your friends and deliver by the first.

> *If you say you'll deliver by the third, wow your friends and deliver by the first."*

"GIVE MORE THAN YOU TAKE"

Have you ever had a friend that only calls you when they need something? Or you know anytime you hang out with them or answer their phone call that it's going to result in you having to give something up? Don't be that friend! Business owners are constantly being asked to donate, discount, "show love" on something by almost everyone around them. The last person they should have to hear it from is their friend. I barely ever have to ask my friends for anything. I treat them how I would want to be treated. For example, when one of my friends launches a new business venture, I support them. If that means buying a piece of furniture from their new collection, posting their book on my Instagram page, or wearing some of their apparel, I do so freely and without them having to ask. I know my support is invaluable so I give it to them in anyway I can. That results in them doing the same for me when the opportunity presents itself. Because good business people (and good friends) know one good turn deserves another. The more you give, the more you get.

37. List of cute things to do with your girls

- Wine tasting
- Sleepover (complete with in-house massage therapist)
- Makeup tutorial party
- Photoshoot party
- Mixology class
- Wine and paint
- Cooking class
- Game night
- Have dinner at a fancy restaurant
- Clothes swap party
- Amusement park
- Girl picnic
- Run a marathon
- Volunteer at a shelter
- Start a book club
- Yoga/Pilates/Spin Class
- Make vision boards
- Go thrifting
- Museum
- Closet purge party (a la Sex and the City movie)
- Go to a museum
- Pole class
- Lingerie shopping
- Karaoke
- Laser tag
- Bowling
- Rollerskating
- Learn to make sushi
- Go for a hike
- Travel to a foreign country
- Search Groupon and find an event
- Movie night
- Girls only football party
- Learn to play poker
- Shooting range
- Take a photography class
- Dinner party

38. Going Dutch: etiquette for splitting bills with friends

You can search the earth and read every etiquette book ever printed. Nowhere are you going to find any definitive rule on how to properly split the bill with friends. Here's my take on it though:

- If I invite the friend out to dine – especially if it's because I'm celebrating something, or I want to pick their brain – I always pay the entire bill. In my opinion, it's poor taste to invite someone somewhere and make him or her pay. If they offer to pay, I tell them they can leave the tip.

- If it's a mutual decision to go eat and it's three or less people including you, it's totally fine for you to split the bill three ways. You can either ask the waiter for separate checks or you and your friends can split the bill equally. Now let's say your friends order lobster, filet mignon, Dom Perignon and dessert, but you only had a small side salad and water, should you still be responsible for a third of the bill? My answer is no. In this instance it's perfectly fine to put a $20 on the table and say, "This should be enough to cover my salad and tip, right?" Of course, the question is rhetorical, but it just makes it known to everyone at the table in a respectful manner that you won't be financially responsible for the frivolous behavior you didn't partake in. Now, if the difference between you paying for your portion or you splitting the bill equally amongst friends is only a few dollars; please don't be that person that is adamant about only paying what you owe. It's tacky to be at the table arguing over a couple dollars and cents.

- For outings including more than three people, you should have a designated person in your party that collects everyone's money and presents it to the waiter. Asking the waiter to split a bill between ten people is an absolute no. Some places won't even do it. So if you're going to do dinner with a large party, encourage everyone to bring cash; let the one friend do the math on what's owed and figure it out before the waiter comes back to retrieve the payment.

39. Friend versus Foe: how to tell the difference

The best indicator to gauge if someone is a friend, or foe is your gut. Your gut is there for a very good reason. It's to keep you safe. The problem is that a lot of us are scared to listen to it. When a friend is no longer a friend, you'll start to feel anxious around them. You won't feel as comfortable with them as you used to be. Those "are they out to get me" questions will start popping up in your head. For me, when a friend starts taking way more than they are giving, it's over. If you only hear from them when they need something, or if they do something to betray your trust, they are not truly, a friend.

As I said before, friendships are supposed to be mutually beneficial. They gain as much from the friendship as you do. It's not always all about them. Don't get me wrong, mutually beneficial doesn't mean 50/50 all the time. Sometimes your friends will be in positions to where they need you more than you need them. Maybe they're going through a breakup. Maybe they lost a family member; or maybe they've been laid off from work. In these instances, it may be an 80/20 situation; but so long as they'll be there for you when you need the ratio to skew to 20/80, the friendship is solid.

> " *When a friend is no longer a friend, you'll start to feel anxious around them.*"

> ❝ *If you're more sad than happy in a situation, it's time to get out.*❞

40. Cut them off: knowing when to terminate an unhealthy friendship

I had this one friend who I was so adamant about being there for her that her problems soon became my problems. Every time she had a fight with her husband, she was calling me, coming over to cry on my couch, or making me call him on three way so she could mute her phone to hear what he says – childish, I know! Her behavior wasn't that stable either, she would drink excessively and pop pills to cope. She'd stay out long hours of the night at random clubs just because the thought of going home to her husband caused her anxiety. At first I was an ear when she needed to talk. I'd constantly preach to her about the dangers of alcoholism and drug abuse. The more I'd try to help, the worse she became. Eventually, she became verbally abusive towards me.

I distinctively remember one night her yelling at me and calling me ugly because I refused to go to the club with her. I started waking up in the middle of the night with nightmares that my husband was cheating on me. The crazy part is I wasn't married. I didn't even have a boyfriend at the time. I literally was losing sleep. I too became depressed, bitter and angry. Sadly, I had no legitimate personal reasons to be feeling any of those emotions, but I was feeling them all. It gets to a point where you feel yourself sinking. If you're more sad than happy in a situation, it's time to get out. You can't save everyone; and the last thing you want to do is drown trying to save a friend that isn't ready to be saved.

CHAPTER 7

Dating

  " Single isn't a status. It's a word that describes
a person who's strong enough to enjoy life
without depending on others."

—Unknown

41. *How to be single*

No one wants to be single, and society makes us feel bad for being so, especially as women. If we don't have a boyfriend, or husband we are made to feel in adequate. Men are encouraged to find their purpose, fulfill their dreams, and sow their Royal Oats. Women however are encouraged to find a man. The crazy part about it is, the men - being the natural born hunters that they are - are actually supposed to be finding us. Don't be fooled into thinking that you are supposed to go out and find a man; and that if you don't get one, your tactics are wrong. He supposed to chase you – but that's another discussion for another topic (... we will talk about later in this book).

Although your mom, friends, and maybe even your ovaries are telling you that being single is a misfortune, it's really not. Contrary to popular belief, finding a partner doesn't mean you are finding your other half. You are not an incomplete person and you need to stop looking at yourself as such. If a healthy relationship is what you seek, then you need to be complete and fulfilled by yourself before getting into a partnership.

Yes, I'm sure you are desperately looking forward to posting bae on the gram with the hashtag, #CoupleGoals and having someone to cuddle with at night; but it is so important to get to know yourself before you get to know anyone else. Being single is the perfect time to get in tune with you. We live in a scary time when society is so busy trying to tell us who we are and who we should be. If we don't know ourselves before putting ourselves into the world, we are doomed. So instead of thinking about how unhappy you are that you are single, you need to rejoice in the fact that you now have time to get to know yourself and build yourself up so that no one can tear you down. Use this time to take up new hobbies, start a new business, build your brand, travel the world, and learn about different cultures, and meet new interesting people. Trust me, once you're in a relationship and have to begin to take someone else's schedule and feelings into account, you're going to reminisce on the days when you were single and didn't have to think about anybody else before you just up and did something. Don't waste so much time thinking about the future that you miss all the greatness that could be happening in the present.

42. Dating within your means: Don't be a nickel looking to date a dime

Don't be a nickel looking to date a dime. I can't tell you the number of times I've been asked how do you "snag a Baller." Sometimes I think to myself that if these women put as much effort into building themselves up as they did into trying to catch a Baller, they would be balling themselves. I actually didn't get with my guy (who ironically is a Baller) until I myself was already balling; and make no mistake, he snagged me. Not the other way around. I was so focused on being a better me, and building a better brand that I wasn't looking for a man. That doesn't mean that I was standoffish, or rude, or pushing men away who approached me, it just means that I wasn't actively searching. I was focused on being the best form of myself. The better I became, the more attractive I became. Invest in yourself so you can add value to your relationship. I once heard Beyoncé say "You should have your own life before becoming somebody's wife." It's such a true statement. A man is not a financial plan. It is very important to have your own. Don't ever let what a man brings to the table be all that you have to eat.

My man makes a few million a year. However, I like to convince myself that financially he's an average Joe with average income. I do this for two reasons. First, I want to stay focused on hustling, building my brand, and being an asset to my relationship. I just don't see it for me being the kept trophy girl that does nothing but swipe a man's card all day. Long gone are the days where that was something people admired. You're not getting any cool points by being the "baller girlfriend." It's so easy to become lackluster in your hustle when you know someone is financing your life. Personally, I have to trick my mind into not falling for the trap – so I trick myself into thinking he's broke. I actually trick myself into thinking I'm broke too. That's how I stay hustling and manage to live beneath my means. I encourage you to find a purpose and achieve some goals. You'll feel so much better when you do.

Secondly, I never want what a man has financially to allow me to give him a pass to mistreat me. I see so many girls put up with so much disrespect just because their boyfriend is rich and buying them things and paying their rent. Having your own, and not being a burden on your man's pockets will make him respect you more, and cause him to think twice before he does anything stupid.

> ❝ *Don't convince yourself that men are too shy, or too intimidated, or that it's the 21st-century and that women can ask men out on dates.*❞

43. *How to ask a man out on a date*

You don't! Men are hunters, and you take the joy away from the relationship by pursuing them. If a man really wants to date you, he will ask you out on a date. Don't convince yourself that men are too shy, or too intimidated, or that it's the 21st-century and that women can ask men out on dates. The way you start off any relationship sets the precedent for how the relationship will be moving forward. If you start off the relationship by asking the man on the date, (even if you do end up in a relationship) you will find yourself having to ask this man for everything. You will have to ask him to be romantic. You'll have to ask him to surprise you with flowers. Eventually you'll have to ask him to do the smallest things such as holding you at night.

I say all this to say, don't rob a man of the joy of the chase. Let a man approach you. Let him experience the joy from scoring the hottest chick in the game. Think about your favorite handbag. You probably had to save up for it, or maybe you asked everyone in your family to chip in and get it for you as a gift. Regardless of how you got it, you value it because it was highly coveted before you were able to get your hands on it. That's how your man should treat you. He should think about how lucky he is to have you, how honored he is that you're with him, and how he never wants you out of his life. Let him woo and win you. Don't ask him to date you, or to be with you. If he doesn't ask, he's just not that into you. Don't set yourself up for failure. If not him, then someone better will come find you. Wait for that man.

> " *Men do not want desperate, no matter how pretty you are or how big your butt is.* "

44. Preparing for your first date: things to do before you go.

OK, so you've finally got a date. How exciting, especially if you've been waiting a long time to be asked out on a date. Don't let this excitement cause you to build 'The Great Wall of Expectations.' Let's keep it real, before a date most women are already dreaming about the six-month anniversary, planning a wedding, imagining what type of house they will live in, and picking out kids names. I hate to burst your bubble, but every man you go on a date with will not be husband material. Don't set yourself up for disappointment. Go into every date with little to no expectation. This will properly help you weed out 'Mr. Wrong.'

Instead of idly waiting for time to pass by before your date, fill your time with productive activities. An idle mind is the devil's workshop and in your case the, "sprung way too early" workshop. You can't properly assess if a man is really good for you or not, if you've already created a fairytale of him in your head for you to fall in love with. Judge a man by his actions, not your imagination. The best way to keep yourself from doing this is to remain busy until it's time for you to go on the date. Run some errands; get a massage, or a mani/pedi. You could even catch up on some reading. Focus on doing things to keep your mind free and clear from sprung thoughts. Don't lurk his social media accounts so you can learn everything about him. You should learn more about him on your date, not from stalking. The last thing you want is to appear is desperate. Men do not want desperate, no matter how pretty you are or how big your butt is.

45. Keeping it cool: do's and don'ts for first date conversation.

When on a first date, keep it cute, light, fun, and flirty. Honestly, the man should actually be doing most of the talking. Don't feel like it's your job to make sure there's no awkward silence during the date. Let him worry about all that. You just focus on being attentive, polite, and confident.

DO:

Do ask him about his hobbies

Compliment him on an article of clothing he's wearing. "Nice Shoes" or "I really like your shirt," is fine enough. Try not to compliment him on his watch or any other expensive piece of jewelry he is wearing. He might mistake you for a gold-digger.

Do ask him what good books he's read lately.

Do say "please" and "thank you."

Do smile and be easy to talk to.

Do end the date first. Thank him for an incredible evening and tell him you had a good time.

DON'T:

Gaze into his eyes longingly as though you can see the rest of your life in them.

Don't ask him if he wants kids or how many.

Don't ask him if he can see a future with you.

Don't ask him his thoughts on prenuptial agreements.

Don't go on and on about yourself and all the things you're good at. You're not on a job interview. He should be trying to win you, not you desperately selling yourself in an attempt to convince him you're worthy. You already know you'd be great for any man. He will pick up on your aura without you rambling on about it. Be forthcoming; but also be elusive. No need for you to tell him everything about yourself on the first date. Leave him wondering and wanting to know more.

Don't rant about how much of a douche your ex is/was.

Don't ask him when you will see him again. Let him ask you. If he doesn't ask, he's not really that interested in seeing you again.

46. What to wear on the first date

This depends on where you're going. Here are a few suggestions:

Lunch   *Dinner*

Miniature Golf   *Movies*

47. My take on the 90-day rule

There are so many different opinions on the 90-day rule. My personal belief is to wait. Don't get me wrong; I've been on both sides of the coin. My last relationship lasted a year and a half before I broke it off. I slept with him on the first night – it was the first time I had ever done that. I'm typically the girl to make a man wait forever to get the goodies. I don't know what I was thinking in this instance. Maybe it was because I had never done it before. Maybe it was because I wasn't expecting the relationship to go anywhere. He gave me the "player" vibe from day one so I already knew I'd be setting myself up for failure trying to work towards a relationship; so I slept with him under the assumptions that I'd probably never see him again. To be honest, I didn't care if I ever saw him again. He was really supposed to be a "good time" not a "lifetime." Surprisingly, he's the one that pressed me for a relationship. He managed to convince me that all my pre-conceived notions about him were wrong and that if I took the time to get to know him, I wouldn't be disappointed.

It was all good until I found out he was a liar and still 'dating' other people. He swore up and down he wasn't doing anything outside our relationship. It took me a year and a half to confirm that was a lie. Everything about him was a lie actually. He's proven to be the greatest con artist of my life; thus far.

Now take my current boyfriend, he's the greatest man I've ever been in a relationship with. He's overly attentive, overly supportive, kind, and caring (ask any of his past girls and they might not be so quick to offer him such praise – He's somewhat of a reformed bad-boy. LOL). But, I believe part of

"Make that man wait!"

what makes him treat me so well is the fact I made him wait six months before getting the goodies. Well, I can't take all the credit; it was a mutual decision. He and I planned to wait until we got married – we failed at that part – (sorry Mom). However, during the abstinent period, we cultivated a genuine friendship and got to know each other without the confusion and insecure feelings that may arise once a man has mounted a woman. When you're friends with someone, it's harder to hurt them. Because he and I are friends, we don't hurt each other. Had I slept with him early, I don't think I'd be as happy with him as I am today. A man values the things he's had to work for. If the man you're with can't wait 90 days before sleeping with you, he probably isn't looking at you in a 'forever' sense. Honestly, what's 90-days when compared to forever? Make that man wait!

> **" *Loving someone else should never cause you to begin to love yourself less.*"**

48. Enough is enough: knowing when to leave a toxic relationship

Dating isn't always peachy. It's two different people with separate upbringings, moral compasses, baggage, and expectations trying to decide how to coexist without stepping on each other's toes or crushing the soul of the other. Small arguments are expected and reasonable, and you shouldn't always run because of a disagreement; but if you ever find yourself at the crossroads of whether to fight for it or leave it be - the main question to ask is: Is it ruining your self esteem? If the answer is yes, it's time to go, plain and simple! Loving someone else should never cause you to begin to love yourself less. Don't use the amount of time or work you have invested into the relationship as a reason to stay. It is better to have wasted the time already spent and take it as a life-lesson; than it is to stay in a toxic relationship and waste even more of your life. Time is a precious commodity. You don't get it back once you have spent it, so spend wisely.

CHAPTER 8

Relationships

❝ A good relationship is when someone accepts your past, supports your present and encourages your future."

—*Zig Ziglar*

49. *Top three relationship do's & don'ts*

DO:

Support your partner and pay them attention; but still know when to give each other some space.

Compromise. It's not always going to go your way. Don't nag or be petty. Pick your battles.

Communicate. Your partner isn't a mind reader, and you can't expect them to be. It's not fair to them. If you want something, tell them. If you don't want something, tell them.

DON'T:

Forgive your partner for something and then harbor on it. If they do something new to offend you, don't use it as an opportunity to bring up all the mistakes they've made in the past.

Be selfish. A relationship is a two-way street. Keep your one-way mentality off of it.

Think that your actions don't affect or reflect back to your partner. You're a reflection of them so keep this in mind. Don't do things you know will make them look bad or embarrass them.

50. How to balance long-distance relationships and work

90% of my adult relationships have been long-distance. I've become so accustomed to long-distance that it's actually going to be a serious adjustment when my partner lives in the same city as me. My belief is that long distance relationships only last if there's a plan to end the distance. Initially though, your partner should visit you more than you visit him. Guys tend to lose interest as time passes, while the complete opposite is true of women. In the beginning, let the man put in a little work to come see you. Let him have to rearrange his schedule, hire a dog-sitter, and leave work early in order to catch his flight on time. In the beginning phase of your relationship, this will also help you weed out any man that's not serious about you. Think to yourself, how often guys will drop everything to go on long road-trips with their boys, or drive hours to go fishing. If he can do all that for a sport, he can surely do it for you, if he thinks you're worth it. If he doesn't, he's a waste of time. Once he visits you two or three times, you can then visit him once. I would keep the same ratio for the duration of the relationship until the 'long-distance' is no longer.

I thought it would be cool to ask my boyfriend some of these questions to get a man's perspective so when you see 'Ask Bae', the response is his take on the topic. He also told me to inform you all that he is not perfect. LOL

*Ask Bae: **The key to a long-distance relationship is communication. Text your girl often, but don't just text. Call her when you can, and make sure to do a lot of Skype or FaceTime.***

51. Date night: how important and how often?

Date nights are super important. With so much going on in the world outside of your relationship, it's important for you and your partner to deliberately take time out to spend with each other, free from distraction. Take a break from work, the kids, or even just the regular routine of sitting in the house and do something fun. Release some endorphins while enjoying each other's company. Date nights don't necessarily have to be expensive, or fancy. They just need to be intentional. It's nice to form a routine in your relationship that you can look forward to throughout the week. Date nights should be one of those things you look forward to. I recommend doing a date night once a week even when you're married. This will help keep your relationship alive and well.

Ask Bae: Date night is very important. That's the time you get to be away from all the chaos in your everyday world to spend with your girl. I (as well as most of my guy friends) have designated Friday Night's as date night. It's strictly reserved for quality time with our significant others.

52. Meeting the parents: How to act the first time your man introduces you to his family?

First things first, be cool! Don't try too hard. Just be yourself and be polite. This isn't a contest to prove to his family that you're the best woman he has ever brought home. Don't ask them about past girls. You should be the only girl you're concerned about. Clearly if the past girl was "The One," you wouldn't be at the table right now; so let those thoughts about any other woman go immediately.

Cater your attire to the occasion. Obviously, don't wear anything too tight or revealing. You don't have to dress like you're going to church on Sunday either. When in doubt, a nice cardigan over a tee and jeans with heels; or a cardigan over a sleeveless midi-dress will work. If the first time you're meeting them will be at an event, dress according to the dress code of the event.

If the first meeting is happening at their house, bringing a small gift is fine. A bottle of wine or flowers for his mom is fine. Don't go overboard with it though. A $25 bottle of wine or a small floral arrangement will suffice. Don't bring an expensive bottle of wine as it may come off as you trying to show off; and a huge, elaborate flower arrangement will only say you're trying too hard. Some sunflowers or lilies are good. Avoid roses.

Ask Bae: The most important thing to me when a girl first meets my parents is that she is herself. ...and she acts as if she has some home training.

53. When to introduce him to your friends and family?

As I've mentioned before in this book, it's important to let a man earn you. Let him do everything first before you do; so definitely meet his friends and family before you introduce him to yours. Don't ask to meet his friends or family either. Let him suggest it. If he doesn't suggest the meeting, wait until he is comfortable enough to do so. Once you've met his friends, you can introduce him to yours. The same thing goes for meeting your parents. If you have children, it's best to introduce them once you and your partner see a future together. It's not fair to allow your children to get attached to someone they may never see again.

54. 13 gifts to give your guy

Buying guys gifts is a different animal than buying gifts for your girlfriends. There's so much pressure when buying your man a gift and it can definitely get tricky. For one, you want to get him something he's going to like. Secondly, you want the gift to be well received. It would totally suck for him to think you're doing too much, or trying to buy his affection, or worse that you didn't put any thought into it. The earlier you are in your relationship; the more inexpensive the gift should be. Gifts in the first few months should not cost more than $100. As the relationship grows longer, the gifts can become more expensive.

1. If he's into Vino: A Personalized Bottle of Wine (personalwine.com)

2. A Good Book

3. His favorite movie on DVD or Bluray

4. A Box of Cigars

5. 2 tickets to his favorite team (let him go with one of his guy friends if you're not into sports as much as he is)

6. A pair of sneakers you know he'd like

7. Golf Lessons

8. An iPad or a Cool New Gadget you know he would like but hasn't yet bought himself.

9. A Nice Wallet or money clip

10. A trip somewhere nice

11. Leather Backpack or briefcase

12. Something to advance his career or hobby. If he's a photographer, some lenses for his camera would be nice.

13. A gift that shows you pay attention. For weeks my boyfriend kept saying he was going to go to the bank to get some $2 bills for good luck; I ended up ordering him a sheet of uncut $2 bills from the Federal Reserve and giving it to him in an acrylic frame. Not only was he impressed that I paid attention, he loved the fact that it was better than what he was going to the bank to get.

55. Keep it sexy: lingerie guide

Every woman should own a good selection of sexy lingerie; and lingerie shouldn't be reserved for only holidays and special occasions. Sometimes I like to randomly sit around the house in sexy lingerie and give my man something to look at. I do it when he least expects it.

When it comes to lingerie, the way it fits you is a major key. Go for pieces that flatter your shape and accentuate your favorite body parts. Most lingerie stores have people who will assist you in finding the right fit. Keep in mind that all lingerie designers cut their pieces differently, so don't be surprised if you're a different size in different brands.

Matching sets always look best. When it comes to color, you can never go wrong with neutrals. Start your collection off with black, white, nude, and red colors. From there you can begin to play around with other colors. The material is important too. Lace, and silk are always sexier than cotton or micro-fiber. Regardless of the color, style, or fabric, make sure you feel comfortable and think you look great in the pieces. If you're not confident in them, it will show.

Ask Bae: It doesn't really matter to me what kind of lingerie you have on, I'm just going to rip it off anyway.

Ask Bae: The Best way to keep your man is to be the woman described in Proverbs 31 of the Bible.

56. How to keep your man

First things first, understand that it's hard enough just being a man. The world puts so much pressure on men that the last thing a man wants to do is come home to a nagging woman that makes him feel as if he can't do anything right. If you want to keep your man, be a helpmate to him and not a headache. Try to make his life easier and not harder. Pick your battles and don't be a nag. Also remember to constantly be on a quest to be a better you. Try to remain the woman he fell in love with. So many women enter a relationship and get comfortable or "fall off." Men are visual creatures, so keep yourself up. Get your hair and nails done like you used to when he first met you, work out and eat right. Don't get comfortable. As shallow as it sounds, it's so real. Make your man fall in love with you over and over again by becoming a better version of the woman he first fell in love with.

57. Dealing with the drama: tips on how to handle difficult discussions

I don't know a phrase that puts a man on the defensive quicker than hearing his woman say, "We need to talk." I don't know what it is about that sentence, but it is not one a man ever wants to hear. I try not to use it. I've had better success with the phrase "Hey babe, can I talk to you for a second?"

Before discussing anything with your man, take a moment to calm down. Address him respectfully. There's a way to have a discussion without being condescending, demeaning, or flat out rude. Often, we women tend to go at our men on the offensive. If your man has wronged you in some way, you're better off playing on his emotions than in trying to "check" him. Let me tell you one thing, if your man is a man's man, it doesn't matter what you're talking to him about; regardless if he was right or wrong, if he thinks you're trying to check him, he's not going to hear it. He will either flip the argument on you, or zone out and ignore you. Instead of telling him how horrible of a person he is for x, y, and z, tell him how you know he loves you but he really hurt you when he did y. Men are protectors and sensing your hurt, his instincts will kick in to make his woman feel better. You catch more flies with honey. Try the "genuinely hurt" approach before the "you're a trifling dog approach."

Ask Bae: The most important thing to remember when trying to have a difficult discussion is to watch your tone, and to keep your hands by your side. Don't yell at me, wave your hands flagrantly in my face, roll your neck, or get rowdy. Also, don't start of with "We need to talk." That automatically makes me want to find the nearest exit.

> " *But, how "comfortable" is "too comfortable?"*

58. Bonnet talk: The difference between "comfortable" and "too comfortable."

There comes a time in the relationship where you both become comfortable with one another. Think back to the beginning of your relationship. The first time you spent the night; I'm willing to bet you didn't wrap your hair and pull your bonnet out. But over time, you both became comfortable with each other and wearing the bonnet to bed became acceptable. You're now walking around the house with no makeup on. Maybe you've even allowed him to see you with your foundation braids as you were waiting to get a sew-in. But, how "comfortable" is "too comfortable?" I surveyed a few men and asked them what they NEVER wanted to see their woman doing and here are a few of the most popular responses:

1. Change a tampon.

2. Take her weave out.

3. Take a dump while I'm in the shower.

4. Entertain another man that's flirting with her in front of me or get too comfortable with my friends.

5. Fart, burp, etc.

6. Digging up her nose.

7. Eat from my plate in a restaurant without asking me if she could have some first.

8. Clip her toenails in front of me.

9. Stop wearing deodorant.

10. Not showering for days because she is not going anywhere or just chilling in the house.

CHAPTER 9

Career & Entrepreneurism

" Find out what you like doing best, and get someone to pay you for it."

—Katharine Whitehorn

> **" You need to be able to sell yourself in a succinct and persuasive manner."**

59. Getting the job. Things to say at the interview to land a gig.

When interviewing for a job opportunity it's important to remember that you are there to sell yourself. Talk about your good qualities, and what it is that you have to offer the company. Interviewees tend to focus on talking about how excited and honored they would be to secure a position with said company, and all the things that the job can offer them. However, what you should really focus on is what you can offer the company. Don't get me wrong, I'm incredibly flattered when a girl walks into my office and talks about how much her life would change just by the opportunity of working for me. But, what really sells me on the candidate is what they say they can do for my company. Telling me how you will be an asset to my company will get you a lot further in the hiring process than simply telling me how much of a fan you are.

Next time, an interviewer asks you 'Why do you want to work here?' Take the time to sell yourself highlighting your good qualities. Make sure you can articulate this information without rambling and with confidence. This is called an 'elevator pitch.' The premise is derived from the fact the average elevator ride is 20-60 seconds. You need to be able to sell yourself in a succinct and persuasive manner. Being able to say a lot in a few words shows you're efficient. Decision-makers love efficient people and can't stand the opposite. Interviewers learn a lot about you from the things you don't say, just as much as they do from the things you do say. Keep that in mind.

Things To Say During An Interview:

"I'm incredibly hardworking, diligent, and very loyal."

"I know I can be an asset to your company based on my past experience at X Company where I raised the sales in my region by 58% through targeted promotional campaigns and strategic marketing."

"I am goal-oriented and results-driven. I have track record of producing big numbers and I know I can do that and more with your organization."

"Although I take pride in being knowledgeable in a multitude of areas, I am also very coachable and believe in learning something new everyday."

What Not To Say:

"I hated my last job. My boss was crazy."

"I want to work with you because you work with a lot of celebrities and I want to meet celebrities."

"If I work with you I know my Instagram followers will go up."

"I really don't know what I'm doing with my life yet, but I think I can figure it out by working at your company."

"I got fired from my last job at BCBG because the manager caught me stealing, but I don't think I will do that if I worked for you."

I've actually heard all these "What Not To Say" examples from candidates interested in working for me. Yikes!

60. What it's like to be an entrepreneur?

It's amazing, exhilarating, satisfying, and most often times fun. What it is not is, 'a walk in the park.'

Let's say you've decided to take this entrepreneur journey. Of course, you're super excited to finally be following your dream(s). You've seen and read so many inspiring startup stories, and you're just glad to finally be in the number. Maybe you even quit your job to take this new life-path by the horns. Regardless of your situation, you are looking forward to the privilege of setting your own hours, signing your own checks, and maybe signing the checks of a few other people too.

> " *Just because it's your passion doesn't mean it's supposed to be easy.*"

Plain and simple, you're pretty geeked about it. Entrepreneurship is something that you feel you were destined to do—it's your 'calling'; but although being an entrepreneur may indeed be the path your destiny has led you on, there's definitely a lot more to the entrepreneur story than the this-will-all-work-out-the-exact-way-I-planned fantasy that many aspiring entrepreneurs tend to formulate in their minds.

Let me be the first to tell you that it is very rare that everything will work out exactly as you planned. The road to entrepreneurship is far from a straight line. You will meet plenty dead-ends and setbacks along the way. The key is to anticipate them so you can modify and adjust accordingly …and in the long-run, WIN!

Statistics indicate that there are way more businesses that fail within the first year than there are that succeed. I believe it's because aspiring entrepreneurs enter business with unrealistic expectations. Often times, the adrenaline pumping through their bloodstream might cause them to convince themselves that entrepreneurship is easy. They have not taken an accurate survey of what it actually means to be your own boss. I want to use this opportunity to give you a few things to keep in mind in order to help you be one of those successful businesses.

Just because it's your passion doesn't mean it's supposed to be easy. As I mentioned before, this journey will be far from easy; but your passion and love for it will help get you through the rough times.

You are more than just the CEO. In the beginning you will have to be the secretary, IT specialist, and janitor too.

" *If you don't work, you don't eat!*"

Most likely you won't have the capital to hire a team in the early phases of your business, so it is critical to know every aspect and operational task required in your business.

You must pay your dues before you expect change (see what I did there). Don't get discouraged and impatient when things don't happen as quickly as you would like them to. Stick with it and you will eventually reach the pot of gold at the end of the rainbow.

Be disciplined and set realistic goals. Know yourself and your nature when it comes to how you best get things done and plan effectively! Write out your vision, develop a message for your brand, and set realistic goals for yourself—both long term and short-term. Be sure to include benchmark goals in order to track your progress. Map out a schedule that you can stick to, but also allow for a small amount of wiggle room. Say goodbye to 9-5er luxuries like 'sick days' because as an entrepreneur, there's no such thing as paid leave. If you don't work, you don't eat!

The best advice that I can give to an aspiring entrepreneur would be to trust your gut and your instincts. Be very consistent with your message and very focused on your goal(s). Never be afraid to take risks. Go for it, and work smart in addition to working hard. Above all else, remember: If it were easy, everyone would do it. Nothing worth having is ever easy to obtain.

61. *Going For It: To save up or not to save up before taking the plunge into the entrepreneur pool?*

Oftentimes, aspiring entrepreneurs ask me, whether I saved up before I quit my job and if so, how much? I was thrown into the world of entrepreneurship so early that I didn't have the time to think if I should save up for it or not. So I guess the answer to that question would be, no. I understand how extremely difficult and terrifying it can be for some to imagine the thought of just quitting their job and starting as an entrepreneur without knowing when or where your next paycheck will come from. Don't become a victim of "perfect timing." Many times people who wait until they've saved up enough to quit their job and become entrepreneurs never really leave the workforce. There's no such thing as the perfect time, or the perfect circumstance. If you're constantly waiting for the perfect opportunity, you will easily find yourself waiting forever. Sometimes you just have to take the jump and build your wings on the way down. After a few years of being a Fashion Stylist, I actually took a hiatus. I told myself I would take a few months off from styling and just relax. I quickly got bored from having nothing

> " *Needless to say, I was a beast.* "

to do, so I moved to Auburn, Alabama where I worked as a sales consultant at Gold's Gym. Super random, I know! I had no gym sales experience; I didn't even like to work out. But, one thing I was good at was selling gym memberships. I'm a hustler by nature, so when my manager told me December was the hardest month to sell gym memberships; I was completely up for the challenge. She set my sales goal at six memberships for the month of December. In December, I sold fifteen gym memberships. The person in the gym with the second highest sales for that month sold a whopping three memberships. Needless to say, I was a beast. I was so vicious with the sales that after only 2 months, I was promoted directly from hourly sales consultant to the general manager of my own gym. The money was amazing, and the commission was even better. I loved the fact that I knew I was getting a check every two weeks. I loved the fact that if I got sick I could call in and say I was sick and wasn't coming to work, and loved knowing that I'd be getting health benefits and a 401K, and all that jazz. I had all the 9-to-5er perks that entrepreneurs never get, and I loved that. But after six months in this position, I was burnt out and I hated the job. I found myself with a bank account full of money, no debt, but no time to spend the money I was making.

I became so obsessed with selling memberships that I was working 70-hour workweeks. I would go into work at 8am and leave at 9pm on most days. It was insane. I didn't even have time to get my nails done because I was at work before the nail salon opened and still at work when they closed. I woke up one day and quit the job, packed my apartment up, and drove right back to Atlanta. I had no plan; but I had enough money in my account (about 50 thousand dollars) to live while I figured it out.

Well, somehow, I recklessly ended up blowing through all that cash before even coming close to figuring it out. I found myself living in my parent's basement with a pile of newly accrued debt on three credit cards, and only enough cash in my account to pay my $70 phone bill every month. I was screwed, miserable, and depressed. Instead of hitting the pavement finding styling gigs, I decided to find other sales jobs. I needed money fast, and I know with the high turnover rate for sales positions that I'd find a job in no time; and I did.

Ironically, I found a job cold-calling people who were behind on their credit card bills. I told myself I was only going to work there long enough to pay off my credit card debt, and save up some money to move into my own place again. The plan was that I would work at the call center from 8am-6pm daily and then focus on rebuilding my business at night and on the weekends. That plan sounded good; until it was time to execute. I was so tired after being at work all day that all I wanted to do was eat, and go to bed; just to wake up the next day to do the same exact thing. I became discouraged as the weeks passed because I saw myself becoming stuck at that job. I only lasted six weeks before I quit.

Back to being jobless in my parent's basement, I decided to do the craziest thing I've ever done. I called my friend Brittany who lived in Los Angeles and asked her if I could sleep on her couch for a while until I figured my life out. At that point, I had only been to L.A., one time, on a 3-day trip to visit Brittany a year prior. Britt said yes, and so I took $149 out of the $300 I had in my bank account and bought a one-way ticket on Air-Tran from ATL to LAX. I packed two suitcases and left for Los Angeles two days later. I didn't have a car, or a plan, or any connections, but when I got to L.A, I was determined to figure it out. I told myself going back home was NOT an option. Here I am 4 years later, living in a $700 thousand dollar condo in the middle of Hollywood, driving a $100 thousand dollar car, with a penthouse office suite in Downtown, Los Angeles. I say all this to say that, sometimes you just have to put your back against the wall. The people with a plan B, seldom achieve plan A. I gave up on having a plan B a long time ago. I'm focused solely on achieving plan A.

62. How to get started in the fashion Industry with no experience.

The fashion industry is over-saturated and super difficult to get into. Thanks to social media, anyone with the ability to type a few characters into a bio is a 'fashion stylist,' 'fashion director,' 'fashion journalist,' 'fashion designer,' and the list goes on. Although this can prove to be extremely frustrating, you can actually use it to your advantage. Because so many people are falsely claiming the titles without investing the time and without earning the credentials, set yourself apart by doing what they won't do, because it's these type of things that bring you true light. Do the actual work, build a portfolio, create a website, and be more than just an Instagram page. Here are a few tips on things you can do get into the industry without having experience:

- *Intern:* Internships are still the easiest way to get your foot in the door. Find a fashion professional in the fashion division you're looking to get into and apply for an internship with them. Don't be discouraged if they don't have an intern program, still ask. You never know; you might just be their first one.

- *Start a blog:* If fashion journalism or even styling is your main area of interest, start a blog. Make sure your blog is clean and easy to navigate. Take ideas from some of your favorite fashion sites for inspiration. Post consistently and build up a following. Many fashion companies will come knocking at your door once they know you have a site that draws the attention of their demographic.

- *Freelance:* Start small. Research local magazines and reach out to them. Indie magazines do not have the budget to keep editors on staff like the Vogue's and Harpers Bazaar's of the mag world, so they are always looking for freelance fashion professionals to work with. Take advantage of that.

- *Put yourself out there:* Join a site like modelmayhem.com where you can work with other fashion professionals at all expertise-levels to build your portfolio. Once you have a solid book, begin by sending out emails to different agencies, publicists, and managers. You can even go as far as private messaging your favorite celebs on social media. It seems like a long shot, but sometimes it works.

63. Tips on building a brand

Know your brand – You should think of your brand as a person. Ask yourself the following questions:

Who are you?
What's your mission?
How do you want to be seen?
What makes you different?

Once you begin to ask yourself these questions, and the others that will arise in the process, you will determine your brand identity. Do NOT move forward with building your brand before knowing everything about your brand. If you wouldn't build a bridge without hiring an architect to draw up the plans, you shouldn't jump into creating a logo, building a website, etc., until you know for whom you are creating these things. In this case, the 'who' is your brand.

Identify your niche—When building a brand that will last find something that's missing in the market and create a solution for it; rather than join an over-saturated market and try to convince others that your brand is better. Regardless of the route you take, you must- know your niche. Who is your ideal customer? What is your target demographic? Once you know who you are appealing to, you will be better equipped to create promo campaigns and marketing strategies that work.

Don't be a copycat – It's sad that I have to include this point. Long gone are the days where people were ashamed of duping other people's intellectual property. When building your brand, it is ok to seek inspiration from those you admire, but it is NOT ok to copy. Never copy someone's logo, website, etc. Consumers are not daft. They will be able to tell and may look at your brand as nothing more than a knock-off. Nobody wants to be seen with a knock-off.

Be innovative, creative, and fresh— You don't work for a big corporation with a manager hovering over you telling you this is the way it's been done for years. You're your own boss in this instance. Don't feel as though you must do things a certain way because you've never seen it done any differently. Be daring, try new things, take risks.

Be consistent in your message and your tone —this includes everything from the layout of your site, to your promotional materials, to the frequency of your content. Don't be all over the place with your language or content.

Be bigger than social media—It's very important to have a strong social media presence, but it's just as important to cultivate a presence away from social media. Though it may seem that we live in a completely digital era, nothing competes with real-life interaction. It is essential that you find ways to engage with your consumer offline.

Be your biggest brand advocate—You have to go hard for your brand. Live it and breathe it! If you are not crazy about your brand, why would you expect anybody else to be. Passion is contagious. Have some for your brand and watch others become passionate about it as well.

Presentation should be on fleek—The biggest mistake I've seen made by newbies is a sloppy presentation. Just because you're new to the game doesn't mean you have to look like it. Take some time to make sure your presentation: your site, code of dress for your employees, or information packet is A-1. No customer will trust you with their money if you hand them a wrinkled business card that looks like you printed it on your home printer last week.

" *The 'WHO' is your brand."*

Focus on your strengths and hire someone for your weaknesses—Confidence is the key in business, but so is being realistic. Know what you do best and focus on doing those things even better. Then hire someone to do the things you suck at. There's nothing wrong with outsourcing.

Aim for long-term engagement with your following—You will never build a brand by constantly hopping from one get rich quick scheme to another. Building a brand is NOT about "looking for a quick check." Your aim should be longevity.

Create a tribe for your consumers—I call my supporters 'SWANKsters', my friend Ming Lee over at Snob Life refers to her supporters as the 'Snob Mobb.' When you give your customers a tribe they can identify with, they will feel closer to your brand and go hard representing for the brand.

Value your reputation—Your reputation can take forever to build, and a second to destroy. If you want to build a brand that will last, operate with integrity. Don't do anything to tarnish your brand image.

" *Whether you know it or not, you are always networking.*"

64. How to network properly

Contrary to popular belief, networking is not some formal thing that takes an announcement in order for it happen. Whether you know it or not, you are always networking. Every person you meet, no matter where you meet them, has the potential to introduce you to another person or a new opportunity. So always be prepared to network. You never know where or when it might happen. Carry your business cards on you always. If you're in fashion, have a copy of your portfolio on your phone. Preparation is the key.

Also, take advantage of "six degrees of separation" which is the theory that anyone you want to meet is six or fewer people away from you by introduction. For example, if I wanted to meet Barack Obama, according to this theory, I should be able to call one person who will call another person, and so on and so forth. When they reach the sixth person, it should be Barack.

When purposefully networking, start with the contacts that you have. If you are looking to break into PR, for example, talk to the people you already know. Put feelers out. Start asking your friends, family, and contacts if they know anyone in that industry. If they don't, they may know someone else who knows someone they can introduce you to.

Look at social activities as the perfect grounds for networking. Sometimes the best opportunities arise from interactions you had in relaxed environments. This goes for dinners, cocktail parties, brunches, etc.

Lastly, don't forget any organizations you were involved in while in college like sororities, fraternities, etc. Don't overlook the alumni office either. Workshops, seminars, and job fairs are good places to network too.

65. How to get your first client.

When I got my first client as a fashion stylist, I wasn't looking. A friend asked me to style the newest artist on Jive Records, and at the time I thought I was doing a friend a favor. To be honest, I didn't even think I would be getting paid. I completed the task as if I had been styling forever because I am good at adapting to any situation I am in; but the real work came after that gig. I had to learn how to get more clients.

The first thing I did was build my portfolio. I found photographers and models to do test shoots with. I was trading my services for portfolio images and credits on my resume. Initially, you may have to do this as well. If you're just getting started in whatever field, your first gig may be unpaid and solely for the experience. Don't frown upon these humble beginnings. Put the work in early and you will soon reap the harvest of the seeds you sow.

Cold calling and emailing is a great way to solicit for clients. Just make sure your presentation is on point and your tools are in order. Even if your resume isn't long, still have one; and don't be afraid to put something on your resume just because you didn't get paid for it. If you gained experience from it, it still counts.

> " *If you're just getting started in whatever field, your first gig may be unpaid and solely for the experience.*"

66. How to hire good employees.

So business is booming and it's time to bring on some staff to help with the workload. This is an awesome problem to have! Learning how to hire great people is just as important as soliciting new customers. Your employees are an extension of your business so hiring properly is vital.

> " *Hire people you will enjoy being around everyday.*"

First, make sure you're hiring people you need. In my years as a business owner, I have come across candidates that were incredible hires; just not for my needs at the time. You must stay focused. If you know your business is in dire need of an in-house graphic designer, stay focused on filling that position. If a great marketing officer walks in your office but that's not what you need, you need to pass on them. What's the point in hiring someone who will increase your businesses exposure and boost your sales if you don't have a graphic designer in house to create the content you're selling? Entrepreneurship is about strategy. Keep the marketing candidates resume on file and circle back to them once your business is ready for them. If they are no longer available, someone else will come along. Don't be so scared of missing out on great candidates you don't need that you become unable to hire the ones you do.

Secondly, seek out people that are skilled. At one point in my life, I would hire people just because I figured having someone is better than having no one. Let me tell you first hand, that mentality is a big mistake. It's better to have an unfilled position than it is to fill it with someone who will eventually put a dent in the reputation of your business because they are unskilled or just don't have the appropriate knowledge.

Lastly, hire people you vibe with. As petty as it may sound, if something about a candidate annoys you during the interview process, that thing will not go away once you hire them. Hire people you will enjoy being around everyday. If you can't stand someone from the beginning, they are not a good fit for your brand. Period!

67. How to handle the competition.

My answer to this is simple. You mind your business, literally. There is always going to be competition regardless of the field you are in: whether you're in the corporate workforce or if you're an entrepreneur. There's always going to be someone going after the same promotion you've been busting your butt for, or a competing company that is doing everything humanly possible to attract your customers. What you do is, you face forward. Focus on how your brand can be better today than it was yesterday; NOT on how you can be better than 'Company Y.' If your focus is on being better than someone else, you will only go as far as that person. If you focus on being a better you, the heights you reach are limitless. I like to use the windshield analogy. The windshield is huge for a purpose. It's because that's where your focus should be. Your competition is the side-view mirrors; you should only peek at them when you are getting ready to change lanes; and even then, it should only be for a quick second. If you drive your car with the side-view mirrors dominating most of your vision, you are bound to crash.

68. How to handle copycats.

I feel like if anybody is best suited to answer this question, it is me. I've had celebrities and 'influencers' alike copying what seems like my every move: from my hair, to my nails, to the type of content I post on my social media, to my pop-up shop designs. There is always someone behind me playing 'Miss (and mister) Me Too.' I can't lie, it bothered me initially and I felt like I couldn't express my individuality without some popular person coming behind me and stealing my whole swag. But, then I realized this was something to actually be proud of. Nobody wants to copy something whack. The fact so many people are copying me actually now boosts my self-esteem. I learned to stop thinking of it as a negative, and started seeing it for the positive it really is. Now, I work overtime to stay ahead of the game and constantly be fresh and innovative. So that's my answer. The best way to handle the copycats is to stay ahead of them. Their best ideas are your old ideas. Don't let it deter you from greatness. Do you, and let them do you too!

 I've had celebrities and 'influencers' alike copying what seems like my every move."

69. Helpful apps for every starting entrepreneur

eCommerce Apps

- Shopify
- PayPal
- Square

Social Media

- Instagram
- Twitter
- Facebook Pages Manager
- Snapchat
- Periscope
- Pinterest

Business & Productivity

- SignEasy
- Dropbox
- EverNote
- Expensify

Lifestyle

- Uber
- Waze
- Postmates
- RescueTime

Photography

- Photoshop Mobile
- Camera+
- Enlight
- Big Lens

70. Books Every Entrepreneur Should Read

"Normal Gets You Nowhere" *by Kelly Cutrone*

"Who Moved My Cheese" *by Spencer Johnson*

"The Instant Millionaire" *by Mark Fisher*

48 Laws of Power *by Robert Greene*

"Before You Do" *by T.D. Jakes*

"The Secret" *by Rhonda Byrne*

"Girl Boss" *by Sophia Amoruso*

"You, Inc: The Art of Selling Yourself" *by Harry Beckwith & Christine Clifford*

"How To Win Friends & Influence People" *by Dale Carnegie*

"The Alchemist" *by Paulo Coelho*

"How To Win At The Sport of Business" *by Mark Cuban*

"Zero To One" *by Blake Masters and Peter Thiel*

"Lean In" *by Sheryl Sandberg*

"The Glitter Plan" *by Pamela Skaist-Levy and Gela Nash-Taylor*

"Year of Yes" *by Shonda Rhimes*

"Think and Grow Rich" *by Napoleon Hill*

"Motivation Manifesto" *by Brendon Burchard*

"A Curious Mind" *by Brian Grazer*

"Push: Pray Until Something Happens" *by Jergen Matthesius*

"The Millionaire Fastlane" *by MJ Demarco*

"Financially Fearless" *by Alexa Von Tobel*

"Promote Yourself: The New Rules For Career Success" *by Dan Schawbel*

71. Importance of Goal Setting, Planning, and Managing a Calendar

Fail to plan, plan to fail. I can't repeat enough times how important it is to set goals and to keep a calendar. Successful people are masters of their time. Oprah has the same 24 hours we do; so how is it that her 24 hours produce 48 hours worth of results? I'd be willing to bet my last dime that the answer lies in goal setting, proper planning, and efficiently managing a tight schedule.

> ❝ *I can't repeat enough times how important it is to set goals and to keep a calendar.*❞

Set Goals—Don't just say them in your head one time on New Year's Eve and forget about them for the rest of the year. Write your goals out and devise a plan to achieve them. When setting your goals, follow the S.M.A.R.T format. Make sure your goal is specific, measurable, attainable, relevant, and timely.

Make a vision board—A vision board is a board where you put images of all the things you want on a board so you can visualize and see them constantly. The theory behind creating a vision board is that constantly seeing the images will cause your subconscious to work towards achieving them. I believe in vision boards. They totally work for me. You can make them as fancy, or as simple as you want. It's your board; make it look like the life you want to live. You can put anything on it from your dream house to your dream body. I also like to put a check on mine made out to me with the amount of money I'm looking to make that year/quarter/month.

Invest in a good calendar system—The way you get the best out of your day is by working it efficiently. It's very easy to have an efficient and productive day if you are looking at the day's tasks on a sheet of paper (or on a list in your app). You can then list them by priority and execute. I personally put everything on iCal on my phone. I can access my calendar from anywhere at any time as long as I have an Internet connection. It also allows me to invite my staff to certain calendars so they are aware of my schedule, and we can all be on the same page. Every time I add a new event to my calendar, they get a notification. It keeps us working like a well-oiled machine. I also keep a physical planner in my purse at all times simply because, I am old school and like to write things down. Plus, if by some God forsaken tragedy I lose access to my iCal, I'll still have my hard copy to rely on.

72. My take on contracts

My take on contracts are very simple: Doing business without a contract is like having sex without a condom. You won't know you've been burned until it's too late. Always have a contract! Always get it in writing, even if it's written on a napkin in a fancy restaurant.

> " *Doing business without a contract is like having sex without a condom.* "

73. How to negotiate effectively

My manager, Ashley Fox once told me, "You don't get what you deserve; you get what you negotiate." That sentence hasn't left me since the day she uttered it. It's so true.

The first rule of negotiating is to not be scared to do it. When I first started negotiating my deals/rates, I dreaded every second of the process. I was always nervous I was asking for too much, or that they would think I was greedy, or that they wouldn't want to work with me if I gave them my real rate. I had to throw that fear out of the window, and I did that by realistically determining my worth. I know what my competitors charge, and I know why I charge the rates I do. When you can comfortably articulate to someone what they are getting for the terms you are requesting; it makes the negotiation process easier for you.

Do not base your negotiations on your emotions. Business is business, and personal feelings should be kept far away. Don't get caught up short changing yourself because you don't want someone to see you in a different light. Both sides are negotiating. Don't get left with the short end of the stick because you want to be nice. Nice girls don't get the corner office. That's another book you should add to your list of books: "Nice Girl's Don't Get The Corner Office" by Lois P. Frankel.

Lastly, don't be so rigid in your terms that you become unreasonable. You should have a list of your non-negotiables but also have other things you are willing to bend on. So for example, maybe your client wants to pay you 75% of what you're asking and they want to do Net 30. One way you can negotiate this is by saying, you'll lower your rate to accommodate the 75% they want to pay but the payment is due immediately upon receipt of the invoice (versus them paying it 30 days later), or you can even say that if they want Net 30, you'll have to be paid your full rate. I say all this to say; the goal is continued business. The cost of client retention is lower than the cost of client acquisition, so do what you can to keep the clients you have happy without putting yourself in the red and drowning your business. You still need to make money after all. Just don't be greedy about it.

74. How to resolve conflict properly and professionally in the workplace

It sucks to have an issue with someone at work, but it happens. When you are having a problem with someone at work, you need to resolve the issue as soon as possible and as respectfully as possible. Approach the person directly, or enlist the help of a supervisor in your efforts. This does not mean you should go rat the person out to your supervisor and start a blame game. What you can do is privately say to your supervisor:

"I'm having a bit of an issue with Jane Doe. I'd like to resolve the issue with her amicably so the conflict doesn't begin to affect either of our performance at work. Do you mind being a mediator while I discuss my issues with her?"

It's simple as that. Your boss will respect the fact that you're being mature about the situation, and you simply want to resolve it. Jane Doe will respect the fact that you didn't throw her under the bus or blame her for things you've yet to bring to her attention. When you do talk to your co-worker, be respectful. Name-calling, shouting, or hand-movements are a no. You're an adult. Adults communicate using their words.

Also make sure that if you do have a problem with someone at work, you discuss it with that person and not everyone else at work. Sad as it may seem, offices are similar to High School. Gossip never leads to a positive outcome, and can actually make the situation way worse.

"You still need to make money after all. Just don't be greedy about it."

CHAPTER 10

Finance

66 No one's ever achieved financial
fitness with a January resolution that's
abandoned by February."

—*Suze Orman*

75. Ten Money Commandments

I. THOU SHALT UNDERSTAND A MAN IS NOT A FINANCIAL PLAN.

II. THOU SHALT MAKE HER OWN MONEY.

III. THOU SHALT USE HER MONEY TO MAKE MORE MONEY.

IV. THOU SHALT MAKE HER MONEY WORK FOR HER INSTEAD OF HER WORKING FOR MONEY.

V. THOU SHALT KNOW THE VALUE OF A DOLLAR.

VI. THOU SHALT STRIVE TO LIVE A DEBT FREE LIFE.

VII. THOU SHALT NOT FEAR MONEY.

VIII. THOU SHAT NOT WORSHIP MONEY.

IX. THOU SHALT ENJOY THE FREEDOM MONEY BRINGS.

X. THOU SHALT ACQUIRE MASSIVE WEALTH.

> " *I blew through that savings account quicker than a shopaholic at a Jimmy Choo sample sale.*"

76. What I've learned so far about SAVING...

My parents opened my first savings account for me when I was about 5 or 6 years old. I'm sure they opened one when I was born as well, but they didn't get me involved and active with it until around age 5. They wanted me to learn the importance of saving at an early age. They even gave me the deposit book to write in every time I made a deposit or withdrawal. They never let me withdraw anything so I never used that column. I used to love adding up my balance to see how much money was accumulating in my small little savings account. All my other friends had piggy banks and no clue how much was in it. I was the opposite. I always knew how much money I had.

When I got to college at age sixteen and tasted the first fruits of financial freedom, I lost my freaking mind. I blew through that savings account quicker than a shopaholic at a Jimmy Choo sample sale. It was disgusting. I didn't stop there either. Every check I got would go straight to material goods. I wasn't saving a penny of it.

It wasn't until almost a decade later, in my mid-twenties where I started to revisit the importance of saving. I will say the concept of saving doesn't come easily. Especially, early in your career where your main focus will revolve around paying your bills and maintaining your current lifestyle. You have to force yourself to do it. Saving requires intense discipline; but it will be well worth it in the long run. There's always going to be a rainy day, you must be prepared for it. Think of your savings as your umbrella.

" *Saving requires intense discipline; but it will be well worth it in the long run.* "

Some ways you can begin to save:

- Pay your savings account before paying your bills. If it's hard for you to pay yourself before your bills, then setup an auto-debit that automatically puts 20% of your check in a savings account.

- Some banks will round up all your debits/charges to the nearest dollar and transfer the change from your checking to your savings account. Take advantage of this service – Every penny counts.

- Contribute to your 401K. Many companies will match your contribution dollar for dollar or $0.50 per dollar. Think of it as free money.

- A Good ole fashioned piggy bank. I have a cute jar in my house where I keep loose change, single, five, tens, twenties, etc. There's something about constantly seeing the jar that makes me want to put something in it; and watching it grow is a daily reminder of how important it is for me to remember to save some money.

77. Balling on a budget... How to stretch your dollar

I'm not going to pretend as if we don't live in a society where everyone is keeping up with the Jones,' and I'm not going to pretend like if I tell you not to try to that you won't. So here are a few tips on how to ball on a budget.

Do your own manicures and pedicures. There are so many drugstore products that will get the job done. Anyone that follows me on social media knows I'm infamous for my $250 nail appointments complete with Japanese nail art. What you might not know is before I could afford that; I was infamous for the Sally Hansen nail decals you can buy at your local drug store. They used to cost me $7 and 15 minutes to apply myself.

Cut back on eating out. Instead of ordering a combo from Wendy's everyday, take your lunch to work or eat at home. Spending $10/day on fast food tallies up to $3,650 dollars a year. Imagine what you could do with an extra three grand.

Buy a coffeemaker and ex out Starbucks. Yes, we all love Starbucks; half of us for the actual coffee, half of us for the social status holding that cup generates. But think about what you could do with an extra $1600 dollars a year by giving up your daily Grande Caramel Macchiato. If holding a Starbucks cup brings you so much joy, buy one of the super cute cups they sell at Starbucks and put your own coffee in it in the morning. Problem solved! Money saved!

Take advantage of Sample and Holiday sales. I cannot count the number of times I've purchased a pair of Christian Louboutin's or Giuseppe Zanotti's at full price only to see them on sale a few weeks later in the store. To make matters worse, I hadn't even worn them yet. Nowadays, I only pay full price for Chanel and that's because the Chanel items I covet never go on sale and I know that Chanel will hold its value over the course of time. Everything else, I wait for a sale. You can score many designer items for up to 70% off depending on the sale you hit. Be patient.

For designer deals online, stalk sites like Bluefly.com and yoox.com

Don't sleep on reseller sites like therealreal.com or luxurysnob.com. You can score gently used – and sometimes brand-new – high-end designer items like Celine, Louis Vuitton, Gucci, etc, for a low price.

> ❝ *To have good credit, you must first understand credit and how it works.* ❞

78. Ask Olori: Do I Really Need To Have Good Credit?

The first credit card I got was during my senior year in college from Capital One. They were promoting on my campus, giving away free GA Bulldawg shirts with every application. Yes, I got suckered into a nightmare of credit card debt, seduced by a mere t-shirt – so sad. Nonetheless, I quickly learned about credit and how quickly you could screw it up by not making smart decisions. If you ever want to own a house one day, buy a car, or even land a high paying job (yes, they check your credit nowadays), I suggest you keep your credit in good shape.

To have good credit, you must first understand credit and how it works. Your credit standing is determined by your FICO score. Your score is based on five factors, each contributing a different percentage towards your overall score.

1. *Payment history* (35% of your total score) – This is self-explanatory. You demonstrate over a period of time that you are a good credit risk by making timely, monthly payments on or before the due date. In short, make sure you pay your bills on time! Payment history is the biggest factor when determining your score.

2. *Credit Utilization* (30% of your score) – How much of your credit line are you using each month? The key here is to keep a healthy balance between the amount you've borrowed and your available credit. Having all of your accounts maxed out every month regardless of whether you're paying your bills on time will not help your score.

3. *Length of credit history* (15% of your score) – The amount of time you've had your lines of credit is taken into account when determining your score. The longer you've had credit and been responsible about it – aka, paying your bills, etc. – the better. This is the one instance where not having any credit can hurt you. Lenders want to see that you are able to be responsible with credit and in order to show that, you have to actually have some.

4. *Application For New Credit* (10% of your score) – You need to be careful every time you let a company do a credit inquiry on you. Every time you apply for new credit (like applying for a Macy's charge card to get 10% off your purchase, or you're car shopping and you want to see what kind of rate your loan will qualify for), you're taking a hit on your credit score. If you apply for too many lines of credit, your score will suffer from it.

5. *Good Mix Of Credit* (10% of your score) – Having different kinds of debt is comparable to having different kinds of responsibility. Lenders like to see that you're able to juggle different types of debt responsibly. For example, having a mortgage, auto loan, and credit card looks better than just having three charge cards.

You should always know your credit score. Sites like CreditKarma.com offer free credit reports. You can find out your score in a matter of seconds. I also like the Experian app. Not only do they monitor your score; but they also offer helpful tips on how you can increase your score.

Of course, the ideal position is not to amass a huge pile of debt; but in the event you already have, pay off your high interest loans first. Call your card companies and setup payment plans. Credit card companies are willing to work with you if you're genuinely interested in paying back your debt. The last thing you should do is ignore your debt. It will come back to bite you one day.

79. Scary Money Don't Make No Money

I think I first heard this statement from my father, and then I heard Lil Wayne say it. The sentiment is very accurate. High risk can yield high reward. You cannot let the fear of losing money keep you from making money. Yes, you might make a horrible investment and lose money, but you have to constantly believe you will make it back. That positive energy and effort you're exuding will cause you to subconsciously do everything you need to do to bounce back even better than before. Just make sure to do your research. You can't always guarantee your investments will be good, but the more you know about what you're investing in, the more likely you will benefit from it.

80. Don't put all your eggs in one basket

No matter how great an investment may sound, never put all your money into just one thing. No investment is a sure bet. There's nothing worse than losing all your money because the one thing you bet the house on tanked. Be disciplined enough to spread your investments across several ventures. That way if one fails, you still have others to rely on or bounce back from.

> " *You cannot let the fear of losing money keep you from making money.*"

CHAPTER 11

Social Media

> " Everything you post on social media impacts your personal brand. How do you want to be known?"
>
> —*Lisa Horn aka "The Publicity Gal"*

> ❝ *What is it exactly that you want to prove yourself to be an expert in?*❞

81. How to build a cult like following on social media

The first thing to do is to decide your message. What is it exactly that you want to prove yourself to be an expert in? Once you decide how you want to be seen, you need to determine a plan to post consistently.

Once you are posting quality content on a consistent basis, the retweets, re-posts, etc., will cause your following to grow organically. One person will like your content enough to post it to their following, who in turn will post it to their following, and so on and so on. It's the digital form of word-of-mouth marketing.

You can also create cool initiatives to gain followers. Do a giveaway contest on your page where you have people mention you or post your picture in exchange for a chance to win something. This method will get you some quick followers; but to build the real true cult-like following you desire, it's going to revolve around the content you provide and the people who like it enough to spread the word.

82. *Pick your poison: how to choose the social media platforms that are best for you*

Just as important as creating great content, it is equally important to know where to post it. If you're known for witty one-liners and thought provoking quotes, Twitter may be your main network of choice. If tutorial videos are your main thing, you definitely want to go with YouTube.

Instagram – is mainly for pictures and short video clips. Don't have an Instagram page full of just quotes. People want to see images.

Twitter – is a word-based platform where you express your thoughts in tweets that are comprised of 140 or fewer characters. I like to post short messages there.

Facebook – allows for a wider range of posts. You can post status updates and announcements, pictures, videos, and even sell products via the Facebook store directly on your page. Facebook is still leading the pack when it comes to the number of active users they have; so having a huge Facebook following helps you reach a ton of people.

Snapchat – is great for posting a collection of short (up to 10 second) video clips journaling your day. These clips all merge together chronologically to form what is called a 'story'. Your followers can keep up with you throughout the day by watching your 'snap' every time you upload one, or they can watch your entire story at the end of the day. Each snap deletes after 24 hours so your following is watching your life 24-hours at a time.

Pinterest – is great for ideas and inspiration. People want to know what inspires the people they are interested in and what kind of things they like: from animals, to food recipes, to DIY projects. Post all your quirks on your Pinterest board and let your following be inspired by the things that inspire you.

YouTube – is to me what it would look like if the largest network on the planet let you have your own show. YouTube is all about video content. It's perfect for having a tutorial based channel.

83. Consistency: when to post and how often

The thing about social media is that no matter how popping, cute, or awesome you are, if you go a long time without posting, people will forget all about you. So make sure you're committed to posting regularly and that your posts are in line with your overall brand message and identity. If you are an artist that specializes in nail art, try to keep your page primarily about nail art. A few random posts here and there are fine; but 90% of your content should be catered to your following.

It's advisable to post a minimum of once a day. The maximum number of posts a day is dependent on the account; but don't go overboard with the posts. Posting every hour can be quite annoying if the content is fluff. If you're posting content that your followers are engaged in; then post away. Just make sure it's consistent. Your followers should see something new from you daily.

> " *Just as important as creating great content, it is equally important to know where to post it.*"

" *When creating content, keep the presentation in mind.*"

84. How to create good content

Be conscious and analytical of the types of posts that get the most likes and the most follower engagement. Make it a point to post more of that type of thing. If you notice when you post shoes you get 700 likes but when you post your dog, the picture only got fifty likes, you know to post more shoe pictures. If you pay close attention to the interaction of your followers on your page, they'll pretty much tell you what to post.

When creating content, keep the presentation in mind. If it's a photo you're posting on Instagram, make sure the quality is good. Nobody wants to see a blurry photo or one that is extremely pixelated. Most camera phones take decent quality photos. If your photos are coming out very pixelated, it may be time to invest in a new phone.

Also, be conscious of the lighting conditions where you're filming. Good lighting will do more for your production than filters and editing ever will. You can also look into downloading a few apps to enhance the quality of your photos as well. Sometimes just changing the brightness on a photo increases how dynamic it looks.

When posting on Twitter, make sure you proofread. Correct spelling and grammar are important if you want to be viewed as a professional. The last thing you want is for people to lose faith in your product or services because your tweets make you appear illiterate. Slang and abbreviations are fine, but unintentional spelling errors are not.

85. The #Clapback: how to properly handle haters, negative Nancy's and social media trolls

Haters, how many of us have them? There are some people in the world with nothing better to do than to troll social media accounts leaving negative, nasty comments on stranger's pages. Some people do it just to get your attention or a response. It's for this reason that I don't fall for the bait. When I come across a nasty comment on one of my accounts, I don't respond. I simply delete and block. Being that I have a lot of followers, it's already hard enough for me to respond to all the positive comments on my posts; so why would I waste so much of my valuable time addressing a negative one?

99% of the time I'm completely unmoved by tasteless comments; however, I am human so I do respond sometimes. Keep in mind that when I do, it's an epic, classy read. I'm never nasty about it. I don't curse at them or call them ugly, or anything else like that. I pretty much just make them feel bad for being so uninformed and judgmental. I do this by discrediting their entire argument with nothing but stone cold facts in the way a prosecutor would demolish a lying witness. There's something about killing someone with kindness and the truth that wins every time.

> " *There's something about killing someone with kindness and the truth that wins every time.*"

When you do decide to respond, remember that your brand image is greater than your feelings. Nobody wants to be bullied on the Internet. It's not a good feeling. You have every right to be upset, but you have to be the bigger person for your brand. You don't look cool arguing back and forth with somebody that has 100 followers and a private account. You should be too busy building your brand to have time to engage in social media beef all day. Pick your battles wisely, and respond to the negativity sparingly.

> ❝ *Social media is not the place for you to air out frustrations.*❞

86. Twitter is not your diary

If you're human, then the possibility of having real-life issues is high. However, social media is not the place for you to air out these frustrations. If you just caught your boyfriend cheating for the eighth time, venting to all your followers on Twitter is not the move. Don't take to Facebook to air out how trifling your best friend is or how worthless your child's father is. It is never a good look.

Although it might prove to be entertaining to your followers, that's all it is: entertaining and counterproductive. Your followers will not sympathize with you. They'll laugh about the situation, tag their friends who will in turn laugh as well. Soon enough, you'll be the subject of ridicule on social media.

If you're having a not-so-good day, or nothing seems to be going right for you that week, find a friend, or family member to talk to about it. Keep it off social media. Sadly, many of the people who stalk your social media accounts are just looking for you to fail. Don't give them the satisfaction of knowing what you're going through.

I read something Jay-Z said about not broadcasting his failures when a collaboration deal with Chrysler to create a "Jay-Z Edition Jeep" fell through, and it has resonated with me. He said something along the lines of: the reason why we (the fans) never heard about the deal was because the deal was a disaster and he never broadcasts his failures. This is how I am. I never want outsiders to see me as anything other than a champion. When I'm at my wits' end, I either stay off social media or I take it upon myself to only post inspiring or positive things. I never let them see me sweat. You shouldn't either!

87. Ask Olori: Why Don't You Post Your Relationship On Social Media?

When you're getting to know someone, it's important to make your own impressions of them without the influence of outsiders. I learned a long time ago that the best thing I could do for the growth of my relationship is to keep it off the Internet. I don't make it a secret that I'm in a relationship. However, I choose not to tell social media who my boyfriend is.

For starters, we all have a past and we all change and grow. What if one of the girls

> " *I learned a long time ago that the best thing I could do for the growth of my relationship is to keep it off the Internet.*"

my man used to mess around with back in his immature days is still salty about how their situation was and wants to send me endless messages about how much of a bad guy he is. If I don't know him yet, I'm definitely going to be influenced by what she has to say. This will create some friction in my relationship for sure.

Let's also take into account the girls who make it a point to purposefully talk to others girls' boyfriends. You know the ones who don't think a man is attractive until they see how great he treats his girlfriend. It's sad, but there are really some girls who are like this. I don't need them sliding into my man's DM's.

Thirdly, my boyfriend has a career that causes him to be in the public eye. The

problem with being in the public eye is that people are always watching you and waiting for the opportunity to catch you slipping. When people know who your boyfriend is and have access to him, trust and believe they will be waiting for the opportunity to tell you how they caught him slipping. He could give a girl a hug and walk off, and the next thing you know, they're posting about how they saw your man "hugged up in the club" with some girl that isn't you.

Lastly, couples have disagreements. Sometimes they work those differences out. Sometimes they don't. If you decide to take a break from the relationship, you can do so peacefully. If you break up with your boyfriend, you don't have to explain to a bunch of followers what happened.

88. How to monetize your social media accounts

I once read a meme on Instagram that said, "Having a lot of followers on Instagram is like having a lot of money in Monopoly, it isn't real." I can't lie, when I read it I chuckled wholeheartedly. Anybody who believes that clearly isn't making good use of his or her social media following.

There are two main ways you can monetize your social media accounts:

1. You can sell a product of your own.

2. You can do some brand advertising.

There was a time I called Instagram, "Moneygram'" because every time I would post something whether it be clothing from *SWANKblue.com* or my luxury hair extensions, the product would go flying off the shelves. I even advertise my workshops and seminars on social media and sell out every course, time and time over. Social media can be incredibly lucrative. The first workshop I ever advertised on social media brought in $16,475.30 net, (net means after expenses). That's a pretty penny for a two-hour workshop (think: that's $8,237.65 per hour!). The only place I advertised was on Twitter and Instagram. Social media can be a helpful tool if you know how to use it.

> " *Once you build a following, you become attractive to brands.*"

The second way to monetize your social media is brand advertising and promotion. Once you build a following, you become attractive to brands. They will begin to offer you free products/services as well as pay you to advertise their products on your pages. This could be anything from posting a picture of their product, to fully endorsing it to your following. It's very helpful for you to create an electronic press kit where you briefly describe yourself, the demographic of your audience, and your reach. Be discerning about the types of brands you choose to engage with. Recall your own brand message—does their brand align properly with your brand compass? If not, you should politely decline the partnership. Your overall brand is bigger than an endorsement dollar.

89. Shout out etiquette... How to promote without annoying your following.

Hopefully, you've followed the path necessary to build a loyal following and you are now earning an income from your selective promoting. Once you begin to promote on your social media accounts, it's important to remember that your followers do not want to be harassed with ad campaigns and solicitations constantly. They are following you for all the great content they've become accustomed to. Don't saturate your feed with posts asking them to buy things. You must give more than you take. For every nine non-promo posts, you're allowed one promotional post. Keep that ratio and your followers will not mind supporting whatever you're promoting.

> " *Don't saturate your feed with posts asking them to buy things.* "

CHAPTER 12

SWANKisms

> ❝ Your beliefs become your thoughts, Your thoughts become your words, Your words become your actions, Your actions become your habits, Your habits become your values, Your values become your destiny.❞
>
> —*Mahatma Gandhi*

90. #SWANKism

It doesn't cost much to pay attention.

91. #SWANKism

Never burn a bridge you're still standing on.

92. #SWANKism

The key to being successful is to learn how to stay hungry even while you're eating.

93. #SWANKism

Be careful who you let gas you. You never know who is carrying matches in their pocket.

94. SWANKism

If you keep cutting corners, you'll just keep going in circles.

95. SWANKism

You've got to pay your dues before you can expect to get your change.

96. SWANKism

Blood, Sweat & Tears ...
shed each responsibly.

97. SWANKism

Stay away from salty people. They will raise your blood pressure.

98. SWANKism

One monkey don't stop no show unless the show is about one monkey.

99. SWANKism

Free time isn't really free.
You either had to work
for it, or you're going to
pay for taking it.

100. SWANKism

If you feel like you're getting the wrong answers, it's probably because you're asking the wrong questions.

CHAPTER 13

How to be a Unicorn

> " Unicorns are awesome. I am awesome. Therefore, I am a Unicorn."
>
> —*Unknown*

IOI.

BEING A UNICORN MEANS you are confident and completely in love with yourself. You're not narcissistic or rude. You genuinely believe that in order to love everyone else wholeheartedly you must know how to love yourself first – and you're not ashamed of that. You might not be the funniest, smartest, or even prettiest girl in the room, but you carry yourself as though you are. You are gracious, humble, and kind. You know you're a wonderful person, and you have so much to offer to the world around you. You're positive and optimistic. You are a divine creation fashioned by God to shine. You are unique and one of a kind. You believe in yourself totally, and you're not afraid to SLAY!

I like to consider myself a unicorn; but being a unicorn isn't always easy. Sometimes, I get discouraged and doubts and fears sink in. However, I've found ways to reset myself mentally, especially when my morale is low and I'm finding it hard to stay motivated to fulfill my purpose.

When it comes to what keeps me motivated, I can categorize my list into two things. The first is my faith in God. I'm insanely obsessed with the Bible verse Jeremiah 29:11 which states: "'For I know the plans I have for you,' declares the Lord, 'plans to prosper you and not to harm you, plans to give you hope and a future.'" Whenever I'm feeling down and I'm at my wits end, I always reflect back on this scripture. I truly believe that God's plan for me is better than my own. If something isn't going my way, then it's probably not the way God wanted it to happen. So instead of quitting, I go back to the drawing board and figure out another way to achieve my goal.

The second thing that keeps me motivated is having a positive attitude. I've learned to see the beauty in everything. My mind is trained so well that I've noticed I actually find it quite difficult to use the word "ugly." This positive attitude helps me focus on every good thing that has happened in my life so far and the awesome things I can accomplish if I just stick with the task at hand. I also reflect on past accomplishments and acknowledge the fact that the task wasn't easy, I just got better. You only get better by sticking with it.

Quitters never win, and winners never quit. If you're having a hard time staying motivated, start a blessings jar. A blessings jar, is a jar that you keep small sheets of paper or post-it notes with your accomplishments in. Get a jar – decorate it if you like – and every time something good happens to you – no matter how big or small – write it down on a piece of paper and put it in the jar. I can't tell you the number of times a surge of new motivation has come over me after opening the jar and reading my many small and big victories.

> " *If you're having a hard time staying motivated, start a blessings jar.*"

Acknowledgements

God – duh!

Mom & Dad – You both have pushed me from birth to strive for greatness. You've been the best parents any child can ask for, and I wouldn't be half the person I am today without you both. I love you two immensely. Thank you for all you have done.

Jo – You are the first best friend I ever had. You're also the first assistant, marketer, promotional manager, damn near every position in my company that I ever had too. Even though at the time I wasn't successful enough yet to pay you, you worked as if you were earning seven figures. Thanks for believing in me even when I didn't believe in myself. Thanks for always seeing way bigger goals for me than I do myself; even though I make it seem like it gets on my nerves. LOL. I love you brother. Here's to your '2011 Prophecy'.

Sai – I'm so thankful to have you. Thanks for always being there for me, putting up with my insane attitude and temper tantrums, and for loving me wholly and unconditionally. I love you just as much. You're my favorite little sister. ...By the way, you would still be my favorite sister if I had another sister besides you. LOL. LPG Baby!

Ashley Fox – Ash, Oh Ash. I don't know where to begin. You are truly a God-send. I thank you for being so trustworthy in an industry that makes it hard to trust people. I feel extremely blessed to have found a manager that shares the same moral compass and values as me. Not only are you the most important member of my team, you've proven to be a true friend and confidante. Love you Ash.

Bae – You are the quintessential definition of the right place at the right time. You found me when I wasn't looking. You're everything I never knew I needed. You inspire me to be great and challenge me to be better all while praising me for being me and making me feel perfect just the way I am. You make me laugh so much that these new smile lines in my face are ruining the resting b-tch face that I took years to master. LOL. You're so magical to me. I daydream about you in colors that don't even exist yet. I love you from the top and bottom of my heart. You're my best friend.

All My Supporters – You buy my clothes on SWANKblue.com, you attend my workshops, re-tweet my press links, and like my pics. I would just be a regular-smegular girl from Atlanta, GA without you all. I thank you for loving me and treating me like royalty.

To my past me – I'm so grateful for the lessons your triumphs and failures alike have taught me.

Find Olori Swank

Website – www.OloriSWANK.com

eBoutique – www.SWANKblue.com

Instagram, Twitter, Snapchat - @OloriSWANK

Facebook – Facebook.com/OloriSWANK

For Press
press@OloriSWANK.com

For Bookings
Ashley Fox, AFoxGroup@me.com